Guarding The Treasured Lands

The Story of the National Park Service

BY ANN AND MYRON SUTTON

Steller of the North

Nature on the Rampage

Exploring with the Bartrams

Journey into Ice
Sir John Franklin and the Northwest Passage

GUARDING
THE TREASURED LANDS

The Story of the National Park Service

By Ann and Myron Sutton

J. B. LIPPINCOTT COMPANY
PHILADELPHIA AND NEW YORK

The authors extend their grateful thanks to the National Park Service, United States Department of the Interior, for all photographs except for those on page 38, Ann and Myron Sutton; page 40, courtesy of the Union Pacific Railroad; page 47, courtesy of the Thomas Alva Edison Foundation; pages 131 and 132, courtesy of the Federal Information Department, Salisbury, Rhodesia; and page 134-5, courtesy of the Canadian Government Travel Bureau.

To Louis Schellbach

park naturalist, from two of many he inspired.

Foreword

I grew up in a state that now has two national parks, a national memorial, two national recreation areas, and fifteen national monuments, and I long ago came to know and respect the men and women of the National Park Service.

Since those boyhood days in Arizona, I have been to parks in all parts of our country, and have never ceased to admire the work and spirit of these guardians of the scenic lands that are a special national treasure.

As Secretary of the Interior it has been a privilege to work very closely with the National Park Service in the common cause of conservation. In this book you will see why. For this is a biography of a bureau and its people, a great Federal agency dedicated to conserving the natural, historic, and recreation resources of America.

STEWART L. UDALL
Secretary of the Interior

Preface

"Sir, how can I be a ranger?"

"Say, ranger! What on earth do you people do out here in the wilderness?"

We have been asked these questions a thousand times, and in the press of public service have never been able to answer fully. To do so would require a book—and that is the purpose of this one.

We have tried to give an idea of how the National Park Service was created, what life is like in the wild and scenic places, as well as the great historic treasures of the nation, and how would-be rangers, naturalists, historians, archeologists and others prepare themselves for lifelong careers.

We cannot thank sufficiently the hundreds of persons inside and outside the Department of Interior who have helped in the preparation of this book. Were we to name even one, the others could conclude that we had forgotten them. Far from it. We are more grateful than we have space to say.

For years we have shared with our colleagues in the National Park Service some memorable days on the trail, nights in the mountains, and stories around the campfire. It is a pleasure to be associated with them, to share their pride and hopes, and to help preserve this nation's heritage for all time and for all people.

ANN AND MYRON SUTTON

Contents

1 · A Ranger's Life

LET US IMAGINE that a boy is trapped on the edge of a thousand-foot cliff. It could be any cliff, in almost any national park, any summer. He clings precariously to a ledge. Below, dizzy emptiness is stretching away to the floor of the valley.

The boy cannot move. He doesn't dare to; one slip and his last foothold will be gone. He hardly dares to breathe.

Above him, a man in a harness of rope and climbing gear inches slowly down the face of the rock. The man's forehead is wet with sweat and his gray shirt is covered with smudges of rock dust. On his shoulder is the familiar arrowhead patch of the United States National Park Service.

Between him and the boy still lie a hundred feet of granite cliff. Looking down, he can barely see the top of the boy's head, motionless, pressed against the rock. Beyond that there is nothing but space . . . and far below, the floor of the valley.

The ranger had left the valley early that morning. People had gathered before dawn to watch. All night he and his teammates had gotten their ropes and harness and climbing gear ready, and prepared for the ascent. They had a stretcher, too, in case it was needed.

The ranger clearly remembered that look in the eyes of the mother and father—a silent plea of desperation to save their son. You couldn't forget a look like that.

Time was passing and the boy would be weakening. They had to go a roundabout way so as to get on the rim directly above the boy. At the first hint of dawn, they started up the trail.

Yesterday the ranger had been on duty at the entrance station. "Good morning, sir. Your first trip to the park?" He smiled as he always did when a car drove up, then handed a booklet to the man inside. "Any firearms?" He received the entrance fee and returned a permit.

"No."

"Thank you, sir. Good luck and have a good trip!"

The man said thanks and smiled and the ranger waved him on. The next car arrived . . .

That was life at the entrance station. The day before that he had been on a horseback trip to Lake Isabel to check on camping conditions. The day before that he had taken the king of a distant country on a tour to Farview Point.

Now dawn had come, touching the mountain peaks with a fiery light. As he walked up the trail he tried not to think of what would happen if the boy collapsed before they arrived.

Last week another ranger and he had gone on a fishing trip into the "back country." It was a high wilderness of shining peaks and glistening snowfields. How fresh and clean the air was way up there!

He remembered how he had taken great gulps of it to clear his lungs of the smoke he'd breathed on the Rio Prado fire. That was the hottest, meanest fire he'd ever worked: flaming snags falling, fire jumping the line, whole pine groves exploding at once . . . He'd gone seventy-two hours without sleep on that one.

Well, it was what he'd always wanted out of life—the trail, the mountains, making friends, working with animals, protecting the park so that generations of people could come and enjoy it.

The sun came over a distant rim and caught his eye, breaking into his thoughts. The rescue team moved silently to the rim. On arriving there the climbers went to work.

Ropes had been secured, knots checked, snap links clipped to belts. It was a long way down to the boy and the ranger was not yet sure that he could make it . . .

"Good luck," his buddies had said, almost in a whisper. He'd been on rescues before;. all of them had. It seemed as if some visitors to the park, more daring than others— or more foolish—were always getting into trouble. He'd helped bring stretcher cases out of the mountains before, people with a broken leg, or arm, or a heart attack, or . . . worse.

He had searched for lost children, and dangerous bears, and wrecked airplanes by foot, by horseback, by canoe, by ski . . . What *hadn't* he done?

Now as he inched his way down the granite cliff, he thought how strangely and rapidly the mind worked under circumstances such as this. At the same time every muscle was tense, every movement practiced, every action premeditated. His years of training were paying off. Desperately but confidently he made his way closer and closer to the trapped, exhausted, and nearly paralyzed boy.

"Steady, son. Don't move." His voice was calm and soft. "Don't turn. Don't try to look up at me. I'll come to you. Don't reach out—just hold your balance. Everything is going to be all right . . ."

The silence was broken by the noise of the rope sliding over the ranger's shoulder as he let himself down. His climbing gear clanked and his boots scraped against the granite cliff. A rock chipped loose and fell away into the yawning chasm.

"Hold on, son. Be perfectly still . . ."

The boy quivered slightly, looking neither up nor down, nor right nor left . . . just waiting.

Slowly the gap between them closed, and at last the ranger circled his arm around the boy, clamping tightly in a vise-like grip.

Next day the ranger was again on duty at the entrance station. About mid-morning, after a steady flow of traffic, a lull occurred. A lone car pulled up to the station and stopped.

"Good morning," the ranger said, with a smile. "How are you folks this morning?"

"Fine, thanks," replied the driver, handing over his entrance fee.

A woman put her head out of the back window, looked around for a moment, then said: "My goodness, you rangers live in the loneliest places! What do you ever find to do around here?"

2 · Campfire in Yellowstone

WHAT THE RANGER DOES—and what he stands for—are part of a tradition that grew in the wild and rugged west a century ago.

In the summer of 1862 a wagon train drawn by ox-teams left Minnesota for the gold fields of Montana. Nathaniel P. Langford, about thirty, straight-backed, with dark eyes and bold features, was second in command.

Langford had heard of fabulous natural wonders in the mountain country where the Yellowstone, Wind, and Snake Rivers rise. It was a little known land, inhabited by wild animals and roving bands of hostile Indians ready to destroy intruders or drive them away.

Trappers and mountaineers had been to the Yellowstone country before—John Colter as early as 1806, Jim Bridger after 1820. But everyone knew what "romancers" these mountain men were. Respectable citizens regarded their stories as pure and simple fiction.

Nathaniel Langford talked with Bridger in 1866 and heard firsthand about the "hot, spouting springs" on the upper reaches of the Yellowstone and Madison Rivers. One spring especially was said to shoot more than sixty feet into the air. Langford was not quite sure that Bridger's imagination was fertile enough to make such stories up. Parts of them must be true.

Not long after arriving in Montana, Langford resolved to organize an expedition to the source of the Yellowstone

Nathaniel P. Langford.

River. But every year for four years he was compelled to abandon his plans on account of threatened outbreaks of Indians in the Gallatin Valley—natural gateway to the region.

A group of three armed men, led by a rancher named David Folsom, did make such a trip in 1869. But when Folsom returned to Helena and was asked to speak of the wonders he had seen, he refused. What he had seen, he said, was unbelievable, and since he already enjoyed a good reputation for telling the truth, he didn't want to say things that people would think were lies.

What he told Langford privately was enough. In the summer of 1870, Langford succeeded in organizing an expedition, even in the face of continuing threats of Crow Indian raids.

For five years Langford had been United States Collector of Internal Revenue in Montana Territory, and he was determined that the rest of the party be composed of equally official and well-known persons. When the group finally met, it consisted of thirteen persons, including General Henry Washburn, Surveyor General of Montana and United States Congressman, as well as Cornelius Hedges, a highly esteemed Montana judge.

After the horses were packed and loaded, the party got under way on August 17, 1870, and set off up the Gallatin River drainage toward Fort Ellis. There they were joined by a cavalry escort of five men under command of Lieutenant Gustavus Doane.

Down Trail Creek and over a mountain spur into the valley of the Yellowstone River the party rode, ever alert for prowling bands of Crow Indians. Once they discovered a party of more than a hundred Indians watching them. Each night they posted guards around their encampment, just in case of surprise attack. For four weeks they traveled,

Getting started. Langford's party heads into the Yellowstone country. (From an early drawing.)

riding over ridges, descending into canyons, fording mountain rivers with current so powerful as almost to sweep the horses off their feet. Day after day, they were plagued by rain and snow, sickness, hunger, accidents, fatigue—and the constant threat of Indian attack.

Despite all this, however, the things they saw made the trip a delightful one. Their minds were lifted by the natural wonders of the region—roaring waterfalls, boiling springs, mud "volcanoes," thundering cauldrons, sulfur basins, emerald pools, geysers, rock spires, petrified trees, lakes, wildlife, and canyons half a mile in depth.

"We are all overwhelmed with astonishment and wonder at what we have seen," wrote Langford in his diary, "and we feel that we have been near the very presence of the Almighty."

They discovered and named Tower Falls, Crystal Falls, and other features, and explored around Yellowstone Lake. After this, they headed westward, anxious to get back home and convinced that by now they had seen everything they could.

"Judge, then, our astonishment," wrote Langford in his diary for September 19, "to see before us an immense body of sparkling water, projected suddenly and with terrific force into the air to the height of over one hundred feet. We had found a real geyser . . . (which) General Washburn has named 'Old Faithful,' because of the regularity of its eruptions."

Crossing a geyser basin, they descended the Firehole River until it joined what was later to be named the Gibbon River. At this junction, in a fertile meadow surrounded by forest-clad mountains, they stopped and set up camp.

That night, as the campfire crackled and sent its sparks into the mountain air, they entered into a conversation that

Wash drawing made by the pioneer photographer William H. Jackson, showing the first view of the Lower Geyser Basin of Yellowstone by the Washburn-Langford-Doane exploring party.

was to make history. It is best described by Langford in his journal of the following day.

"Last night, and also this morning in camp, the entire party had a rather unusual discussion. The proposition was made by some member that we utilize the result of our exploration by taking . . . land at the most prominent points of interest . . .

"One member of our party suggested that if there could be secured by pre-emption a good title to two or three quarter sections of land opposite the lower fall of the Yellowstone and extending down the river along the canyon, they would eventually become a source of great profit to the owners.

"Another member of the party thought that it would be more desirable to take up a quarter section of land at the Upper Geyser Basin, for the reason that that locality could be more easily reached by tourists and pleasure seekers.

"A third suggestion was that each member of the party pre-empt a claim, and in order that no one should have an advantage over the others, the whole should be thrown into a common pool for the benefit of the entire party.

"Mr. Hedges then said that he did not approve of any of these plans—that there ought to be no private ownership of any portion of that region, but that the whole of it ought to be set apart as a great National Park, and that each one of us ought to make an effort to have this accomplished.

"His suggestion met with an instantaneous and favorable response from all—except one—of the members of our party, and each hour since the matter was first broached, our enthusiasm has increased. It has been the main theme of our conversation today as we journeyed. I lay awake half of last night thinking about it—and if my wakefulness deprived my bedfellow (Hedges) of any sleep, he has only himself and his disturbing National Park proposition to answer for it."

Langford knew that creating a park could be accomplished only by untiring work. First they had to overcome the disbelief that would greet their description of the wonders of the region. Then they had to convince the United States Congress that the park idea was a good idea.

"Nevertheless," he added in his diary, "I believe we can win the battle."

As soon as the expedition, bedraggled and saddle weary, returned to Helena, its members told of what they had seen. Articles about the park proposal began to appear in local newspapers. Lieutenant Doane completed a splendid report for the military. Langford and Hedges, together with Congressman William Clagett of Montana, laid plans for their park bill, and Langford himself went on a lecture tour to Washington, New York, and Minneapolis.

The following summer, with all this interest being stirred, two new expeditions entered the Yellowstone, one military, the other an official geological survey under Dr. F. V. Hayden. These groups discovered even more wonders, including Mammoth Hot Springs on the Gardner River. They also gained new facts and figures to confirm the earlier discoveries. Most importantly, they returned with photographs—proving to all that the wonders were real.

In Washington, the Yellowstone Park bill was introduced into Congress in December of 1871, and Langford, Hayden, and Congressman Clagett stepped up their efforts to get it passed. Every congressman was personally interviewed and provided with copies of articles about the Yellowstone. Hayden's report was issued, describing the region in detail. Photographs and specimens went on display, and were pored over by congressmen and the public at large.

Within six weeks, the Senate passed the bill. The House approved it four weeks later. President Grant signed the Act on March 1, 1872, thus creating the world's first national park. Not quite a year and a half had passed since Cornelius Hedges voiced his idea around that famous campfire on the bank of the Firehole River.

He and Langford and Hayden and Congressman Clagett could be proud of the result. Through their efforts the Yellowstone region had been permanently "dedicated and set apart as a public park or pleasuring-ground for the benefit and enjoyment of the people."

3 · The National Parks

NATHANIEL P. LANGFORD served as the first superintendent of Yellowstone National Park for five years—all without pay and without funds to run his park.

There were no roads, no railroads, no bridges, scarcely any trails. Illegal hunting was being carried on. As other superintendents succeeded Langford and the park became better known, various schemes were hatched outside to exploit the geologic wonders. Laws to control unsavory practices and proposals were made and repealed. For a while Congress appropriated funds for administration of the park but they were never enough, and finally the situation became so bad that funds were withdrawn. The Secretary of the Interior had to appeal to the Army to come in and take over.

None of this lessened the zeal of Americans to save their scenic lands while they could. By now there were other parks. Even before Yellowstone, land had been set aside to prevent private exploitation—the Hot Springs Reservation in Arkansas (1832) and the Yosemite Valley in California (1864). Yosemite became a full-fledged park in 1890, as did Sequoia and General Grant (now Kings Canyon).

These parks in the high Sierra contained not only wild mountain scenery, soaring waterfalls, and abundant wildlife, they were nearly the last refuges of the giant Sequoia trees—which once had spread across the continent. The only other park to be created by the turn of the century was Mount Rainier, in the state of Washington—a glacier-clad

John Burroughs (left) and John Muir in Yosemite, 1909.

14,410-foot volcano in the wild and majestic Cascade Range.

It happened that in the high Sierra one of the next big forward steps in conservation was made. John Muir, born in Scotland and raised in Wisconsin, had come to the California mountains in 1868. There he fought so hard and so eloquently for the establishment of Yosemite National Park that he became known as "John of the Mountains," and was respected the world over.

In 1903, President Theodore Roosevelt visited the Sierras and John Muir went with him into the wilderness. They rode horseback along the trails, talked around the campfire, and slept under the giant sequoias. While Roosevelt listened, Muir preached his eloquent brand of conservation.

"Through all the wonderful, eventful centuries," Muir would have said, "God has cared for these trees, saved them from drought, disease, avalanches, and a thousand straining, leveling tempests and floods. But He cannot save them from fools—only Uncle Sam can do that."

This experience was, in Roosevelt's words, "the grandest day of my life!"

That same year, Roosevelt, accompanied by the eminent naturalist, John Burroughs, spent sixteen days at Yellowstone. The President later called a conservation conference in Washington, and from this new movement the National Park Service was to grow.

Having a conservation-minded President in the White House, it is no wonder that great strides were made for the parks. As soon as Congressman John Lacey of Iowa had promoted and successfully put through his "Act for the Preservation of American Antiquities," Roosevelt had what he needed. This Act empowered the President, by public proclamation, to declare as "National Monuments" scientific and historic landmarks on public land, thus preserving them from damage.

No sooner said than done. Under the Antiquities Act, Roosevelt established Devils Tower, in Wyoming, as the first National Monument. He followed this immediately by establishing Montezuma Castle, Petrified Forest, and El Morro National Monuments in the desert Southwest.

Meanwhile, management of the parks was going from bad to worse. In 1886 the military had assumed control in Yellowstone. Cavalry detachments also moved into other parks, and to some extent the poaching and other illegal practices were reduced. But some of the parks and monuments were being run by the War Department, some by the Department of Agriculture, some by Interior.

Worse yet, there were no policies to guide the superintendents and their staffs—not even a central office to lay down objectives for park use.

A Cavalry sergeant beside his quarters in Yosemite National Park, 1896.

The Interior Department certainly seemed a logical place for such an office. Interior had been created in 1849 as the result of a need for a "domestic" department to handle the growing national riches coming from the conquest of the West. The Department of Interior already consisted of a General Land Office, an Office of Indian Affairs, Geological Survey, Bureau of Reclamation, and Bureau of Mines.

Why not a bureau of parks?

Nobody had a plan for creation of the parks themselves. Groups of local people here and there got national support to save their scenic wonders, and so it went, state by state, helter-skelter. In 1902 Platt and Crater Lake National Parks were established, Wind Cave in 1903, Mesa Verde in 1906, and Glacier in 1910.

By 1912, moreover, nearly forty national monuments, reserves, battlefield parks, and miscellaneous sites had been set aside. Among these were such well known places as Muir Woods, near San Francisco, Rainbow Bridge, in Utah, and the Civil War battlefields at Shiloh, Antietam, and Gettysburg.

That same year, President William Howard Taft, who knew very well that some kind of organization had to be set up if the parks were to be properly preserved, urged Congress to create a National Park Service. Bills for this purpose were introduced then, and again in 1913, but they did not succeed.

As if to underscore the urgency of the situation, a water supply reservoir and power generation plant were authorized to be built in the magnificent Hetch Hetchy Valley of Yosemite National Park. For nearly ten years John Muir, the Sierra Club, and many others fought valiantly against this proposal.

They lost, and their defeat demonstrated that if the parks were not to be chewed away bit by bit, if the great scenic wonders were to be preserved for all time—then guardians must be appointed over them. Canada had a bureau of parks that was working very well. Why not the United States?

Franklin K. Lane, then Secretary of the Interior, did the best he could. He placed an Assistant Secretary in general charge of park administration, and got authority and money from Congress to hire some general superintendents and a landscape engineer. But it was not enough. Even Lane himself said, "If the railroads were conducted in the same manner as the national parks, no man would be brave enough to ride from Washington to Baltimore."

He kept on trying, and with the coming of war in Europe —cutting off pleasure travel in that direction and stimulating a "see America first" attitude at home—he saw a chance to get a parks bureau proposal through Congress at last.

It was while Lane was looking for an energetic idea-man to help promote the parks bill in Washington that he got a

letter from a University of California fellow alumnus and
friend named Stephen T. Mather.

Mather was indignant at the way the parks were being
run and he said so. Whereupon Secretary Lane replied:
"Dear Steve, if you don't like the way the national parks
are being run, come on down to Washington and run them
yourself."

4 · Steve Mather's Legacy

RARELY HAS THERE BEEN so perfect a case of the right man for the right job. Stephen T. Mather—forty-seven years old, hair prematurely gray, blue eyes penetrating, a shade over six feet tall—had long been an outdoor enthusiast. In California he had "climbed the mountains to get their good tidings," as John Muir had said. Mather knew Muir, and belonged to the Sierra Club. Most of all, Mather was a hard worker with a day and night flow of ideas. He was also a millionaire. For twenty-two years he had built a fortune in borax manufacturing (he originated the "20-Mule-Team" brand) and now, even though he had a horde of interests, he was restless. The park job looked good and he took it.

A great handshaker, friend to all, and fast mover—his biographer calls him a human whirlwind—that was the kind of man Lane needed. When Mather got to Washington, he faced a task that would have floored a lesser man, but he waded right in.

First thing was to get the Act passed creating the National Park Service, and to do that he had to arouse public interest so that congressmen would listen.

This he did by organizing wide publicity, using the most effective "convincers" he had: pictures of the parks and the wildlife therein. He called a national parks conference and later helped to dedicate the new Rocky Mountain National Park.

Another thing he had to do was make the parks easy to get into. At this time it was required that visitors' automobiles in Yosemite National Park be chained to logs and

30

Auto caravans, once very popular, left headquarters under a ranger's guidance. Along the roadside, visitors parked their cars and accompanied the ranger to nearby points of interest. Such programs are rare today because of high volume of traffic.

the keys turned in at headquarters. In Yellowstone, cars were banned altogether.

Mather knew that even though autos seemed dangerous, they were here to stay and that free access would invite travel as well as support for the parks. Accordingly, he opened the parks to cars and lent his support to groups promoting "park-to-park highways." He invited the House Appropriations Committee—which was then touring the West and whose support was crucial to the National Park Service bill—to Yellowstone and Yosemite, and even roomed with the Committee chairman on a good part of the trip.

The *Saturday Evening Post* glamorized the parks through favorable editorials and popular stories by such authors as Emerson Hough (who wrote *The Covered Wagon*) and Mary Roberts Rinehart (who wrote *Tenting Tonight*). It also called attention—not always favorably—to their management. Strong support came from newspapers, too, including those of such diverse readership as the *Brooklyn Eagle*, and the *Denver Post*. Then in April, 1916, the *National Geographic Magazine* got out an issue devoted largely to the national parks, with magnificent photographs, some in color. And just in time. The issue appeared during Congressional hearings on the Park Service bill.

That bill was drafted and redrafted by Mather and a group of influential conservationists, and just at the right moment was introduced. With 1916 an election year, talk of economy filled the air. Some congressmen opposed the bill. Others wanted to restrict it. Nevertheless, it passed the House, and then the Senate—but with amendments.

A conference was called to straighten out differences, and a compromise bill resulted. Even this met opposition. But finally the Act was passed, and President Woodrow Wilson signed it into law on August 25, 1916.

Stephen T. Mather and the Superintendent of Yosemite, 1924.

"There is hereby created in the Department of the Interior," the Act read, "a service to be called the National Park Service . . ."

Another round in the battle for conservation had been won, and the victory belonged to Mather—who became the first director of the newborn bureau.

The rest of the Act was a double challenge. "The service thus established," it said, "shall promote and regulate the use of the . . . national parks, monuments, and reservations . . . by such means and measures as conform to the fundamental purpose of the said parks . . . which purpose is to conserve the scenery and the natural and historic objects and the wildlife therein and to provide for the enjoyment of the same in such manner and by such means as will leave them unimpaired for the enjoyment of future generations."

Use them and save them; how to do both at once was the challenge!

In the National Park Service that began to grow that day, it was Mather's challenge and the challenge of every ranger, superintendent, and citizen around the nation.

Mather built up a publicity program to let the public know what treasures it had in the parks. He labored mightily to improve the lodge and camping situation so as to attract more people to the parks. In part of these endeavors he was helped by the railroads, such as the Great Northern in Glacier, the Santa Fe in Grand Canyon, and the Union Pacific at Bryce, Zion and Grand Canyon.

Roads into remote areas were atrocious, and Mather felt that though a road was an intrusion, it nevertheless ought to be the best that money could build. To get enough money, he constantly coaxed the Congress to appropriate funds for the parks. His young assistant director, Horace Albright, did the same, and when they could find no other money to build the roads, Mather used his own.

The "Gay Twenties" came, and the parks looked better than ever. Two magnificent roads were built—Going-to-the-Sun Highway in Glacier National Park, and Trail Ridge Road in the Rocky Mountains. New parks also came into being—Hawaii and Lassen Volcanic in 1916, Mount McKinley in 1917, Grand Canyon in 1919, Hot Springs in 1921, and Bryce Canyon in 1928. Other park proposals lay before Congress, but they did not succeed until after Mather's time.

Moving like a whirlwind, Mather strove to consolidate the gains made for the parks and for conservation generally. He enlarged some parks, reduced private holdings, organized a national conference on state parks, fought promotion schemes, got assistance from other bureaus such as the Geological Survey, and fell full-length into a battle to save the California redwoods.

His infant bureau grew. Park superintendencies were filled with young and eager men. When he heard of a "nature-guide" experiment at Lake Tahoe, sponsored by a California businessman named C. M. Goethe, Mather in-

Outdoor programs for the public were successful from their start in the 1920's. Here, a ranger guides visitors into the high country.

vestigated, liked the idea, and moved the whole arrangement to Yosemite.

Goethe had seen in Switzerland how effective guided walks along the trails could be, and had brought the idea to the United States. Thus in 1920 the first "interpretive" programs in the national parks began.

In addition to outdoor walks and hikes, the Service's "Information Rangers" organized campfire programs, commemorating that famous campfire in Yellowstone where the national park idea was born.

Museums were also started, not only in Yosemite, but in Yellowstone and Mesa Verde. Mather, wherever he could, enlisted the aid of wealthy philanthropists, and money for critically needed projects poured in.

Suddenly, in 1929, Mather had a stroke that laid him low. While convalescing, he was deluged with mail and good wishes—even from the White House. But his condition grew worse, and the following year he died. The nation mourned as rarely it did for the chief of a bureau, and messages of praise arose from everywhere. The directorship fell to Albright, Mather's protégé, who with all his experience, carried on in the Mather tradition.

In 1933, under a reorganization of the Executive Branch of the Government, sixty-four monuments, military parks, battlefield sites, and memorials were transferred to the Service for administration. So were certain battlefield cemeteries, as well as parks of the nation's capital.

Since that time, with the addition of Big Bend, Mammoth Cave, Virgin Islands and others, the national park system has increased to more than twenty-six million acres, less than one per cent of the land of the United States. (See list of parks and related reserves, page 145).

All this is quite a legacy. Steve Mather would be proud—not only of how the system of parks has grown, but of that prideful organization he fought so hard to make good—the National Park Service.

As one of his contemporaries, a member of Congress, said when Mather died: "There will never come an end to the good he has done."

5 · The Wild Places

STEVE MATHER, with all his vision, would not in the least be surprised to see what the national park system has become today. Consisting of more than two hundred areas, it runs the scale of variety from A to Z and it is likely to grow as the demands of the people increase. He would also be delighted at the rising number of visitors to this system—a number that is expected to exceed two hundred million a year by the end of the twentieth century.

But visiting the parks is one thing; living in them is another. What is it like to live in the parks all year? Or, as the lady asked the ranger at the entrance station, "What do you find to do around here?" The answer is that there is plenty to do, and it is done in some of the finest places on earth.

Take, for example, our days at Montezuma Well, part of Montezuma Castle National Monument, an isolated outpost in the Verde Valley of central Arizona. The "Well" is a natural limestone sink 470 feet in diameter and from which flow a thousand gallons of water a minute. The water came past our house, a simple frame dwelling set in a grove of cottonwood trees, and made the locality an ideal habitat for birds, mammals, reptiles, and insects. As a result, we were surrounded by the kinds of landscapes and living creatures we had studied and taught about in college.

Off duty we never found sufficient time for all the things we wanted to do. There were always a hundred places in the Verde Valley to explore; we got to many, and heard of more. We took notes and photographs and did research, preparing

Montezuma Well, a natural limestone sink whose walls contain ancient Indian ruins and whose waters attract great numbers of migrating birds.

articles that appeared in national magazines, and writing a booklet on the geology of the region.

Examining old records and prowling with binoculars, we compiled a list of over 190 species of birds of the valley. We recorded on tape the songs and calls of nearly thirty species of birds that lived around the house and at night collected moths and beetles and a host of other invertebrates for the park scientific collections. (Though such activities are performed on a ranger's personal and private time, the knowledge gained helps him to serve the public better when he is on official duty.)

Through time-lapse photography we made a motion picture of summer cloud movements over the valley. We gave talks and showed pictures at local schools. We entertained visitors and visited others. We camped and hiked. We swam in the clear, wild streams of desert and mountain, and tried to turn our hands to oil painting and to writing a novel.

One Christmas we designed and executed our own greeting cards. Another time we made and hand-tooled leather purses, belts, and camera cases to be used as gifts. Collecting gourds and devil's claws and other dried wild fruits outside the boundaries of the park, we painted and strung some brightly colored "charm strings" for friends and relatives.

There were dozens of other things to make or hikes to take and dozens of subjects we wanted to write about—but they had to wait. We never had time. And yet, paradoxically, we can remember the times we simply lounged on the lawn and did absolutely nothing—soaking up that brilliant Arizona sun. The idea was not to drive ourselves relentlessly, but to spend our spare time just as carefully and as profitably as we could, and never let a moment get away unaccounted for.

On duty, meanwhile, there were visitors to the monument every day of the year, except perhaps when heavy rains washed out the dirt roads and these were not repaired for a day or two. Each morning the museum was opened, the flag raised, yesterday's litter removed and trash hauled, and the picnic grounds and scenic features inspected. Notes on any new bird or animal observation were recorded. Then the giving of information and answering of questions occupied the busy summer hours.

On days of lesser travel, plenty of catch-up projects awaited: repair a road or fence, adjust the water pump, build new walls or steps, complete a trail booklet, revise musum exhibits, attend training programs, prepare reports. Here, too, there was never time enough to finish all the public business that had to be done, and at sundown when the flag was lowered, there was always that wonderful feeling that on the morrow there would be plenty to do.

Such was the life of a ranger in a relatively small southwestern desert unit of the national park system. But there were other desert parks and we visited them whenever we could on our days off. They were worth visiting, too. Saguaro and Organ Pipe Cactus National Monuments in Arizona are filled with bizarre and twisted giant cactus and natural gardens of extraordinary variety. At Big Bend National Park, on the Texas side of the Rio Grande, the atmosphere resembles that of old Mexico, and is an ideal place for the

Red cliffs of sandstone rise thousands of feet above the Virgin River in Zion National Park, Utah.

A veil of heavy snow converts Yosemite Valley into a wilderness winter wonderland.

Enjoying the beach in Virgin Islands National Park in the Caribbean.

Spanish-speaking ranger to work and make friends with his neighbors across the border.

The hottest park is Death Valley (134 degrees is the record), but even there the land is not as hostile as it seems, for the winter months and the summer mornings and evenings can be delightful.

Rangers with an interest in the lands of the north, with winters full of snow and ice, may find themselves at Glacier, Yellowstone, Isle Royale, or any of a dozen other places. They may be assigned to Mount McKinley National Park, Alaska, where the highest mountain in North America rises to 20,320 feet. And they might share in a part-time assignment to Katmai National Monument, largest unit in the national park system (4,200 square miles, more than twice as big as the state of Delaware). Skiing, skating, and snowshoeing are in order in such northern lands, and maybe a little dogsled racing, too.

In the United States, snow piles deepest on Mount Rainier (an average 575 inches annually at Paradise Ranger Station) but drifts at Glacier, Crater Lake, and Lassen Volcanic National Parks reach a depth of sixty feet. One of the coldest parks is Grand Teton, Wyoming, where the temperature has dropped to more than sixty degrees below zero.

None of these parks is closed in winter—no park is for that matter—but ranger patrols in most of the snowed-in areas have to be by over-the-snow vehicles, or by ski or snowshoe.

It may well be imagined what winter wonderlands these places are. Such sights as Old Faithful steaming in the deep

Old Faithful geyser in Yellowstone National Park.

blue wintry sky, or ice-encrusted trees on the rim of Crater Lake, or Yosemite Valley draped and festooned with heavy snow, are never to be forgotten.

The Everglades of Florida, and the Virgin Islands in the Caribbean Sea are far, far different in character. In Everglades an abundance of wildlife (birds, alligators, deer, cougar, even the rare American crocodile) makes canoe patrols through the mangroves exciting indeed. In the Virgin Islands, and especially at Buck Island Reef National Monument, are excellent marine gardens for snorkeling and skin diving.

To be sure, the tropics, the desert, and the snow-capped mountains are glamorous. But other places, though less spectacular, hold just as many pleasures and adventures for the ranger and his family.

There is a certain unforgettable charm about the deciduous forests of the eastern United States. In the spring these wild woodlands blaze with flame azalea, rhododendron, mountain laurel and a host of wildflowers that set the mountains "afire." It is an ideal time of year for hiking, and on some of the balds, or treeless mountaintops, in the Great Smoky Mountains, one can witness spectacular floral displays.

During October, the mountains blaze with brilliant reds and gold of autumn leaves, and the air is clear and sharp. It is a time of which the eminent naturalist Aldo Leopold spoke when he said: "I sometimes think that the other months were constituted mainly as a fitting interlude between Octobers, and I suspect that dogs, and perhaps grouse, share the same view."

A hike to Whiteoak Falls in Shenandoah National Park, Virginia, is just what the ranger needs after a hectic week of helping thousands of motorists cruise in comfort along the Skyline Drive.

Shenandoah and Great Smoky Mountains National Parks are connected by the 469-mile Blue Ridge Parkway, a winding, ridge-top road that passes leisurely through some of America's most historic mountains. Here the Southern Highlanders still practice their crafts of old, inspiring the ranger and his family to learn new skills, whirl at square dances, or visit early cabins, blacksmith shops, and grinding mills such as are restored and preserved along the Parkway.

History itself becomes an integral part of park living. Duty at Mammoth Cave, for example, can result in a new respect for the difficulties encountered in the War of 1812. Here, elaborate apparatus was carried into the cave to extract saltpeter from cavern earths, and the saltpeter was then shipped elsewhere to be used in making gunpowder. Saltpeter vats still remain in the "Rotunda," a short distance inside the entrance of the cave.

At Yosemite there was an early mining industry. At Glacier is a long and absorbing story of the Blackfeet Indians. At Acadia one learns of the exploration of Samuel de Champlain. At Cape Hatteras, true tales of sea rescues by heroic coast guardsmen off North Carolina read like thrilling adventure stories.

In the historic sites themselves, where the land is not so wild, park people not only safeguard irreplaceable national shrines, they have a chance to examine original letters, documents, and objects—some of them hundreds of years old—in the normal course of research. Few better ways exist to find out what our forefathers said and did—and why.

The hardships suffered by George Washington and his men in the winters of 1777 and 1779 become more real when you tour the quarters and grounds at Morristown National Historic Park, in New Jersey. There is a splendid library at park headquarters, and for park historians and others, being at Morristown reveals the American Revolution in rich perspective.

As for the war between the states, to stroll across the battlefield at Gettysburg . . . or Antietam . . . or Shiloh is a thrill which, once felt, is never forgotten. Indeed, the historian's lot can be a lively one. Just to protect such hallowed grounds and keep these national treasures safe and sound is a proud responsibility that brings its own rewards. But he can join a local or regional historical society, scout out new leads to the solution of old mysteries, and interview pioneers and other oldtimers. Some historians collect early armor or weapons, some even try to restore and shoot old firearms but this is a potentially dangerous hobby that calls for years of research and a great deal of specialized knowledge—or else the end of the hobby may be a crippling injury.

Sometimes an old bottle or belt buckle or piece of Indian pottery will excite an interest so intense that few but the historian or archeologist will understand why such ado about nothing. But the objects are not insignificant, and the historian and his family may travel to distant cities or possibly overseas and visit with famous people to look for clues. That bottle or buckle or potsherd may hold the key to solving a long-mysterious part of the history of the United States.

Historians and archeologists deal with ideas as well as things, and living and working in the shadow of a great man has its extraordinary inspiration. One example of this is at Edison National Historic Site, West Orange, New Jersey. Here in shops and laboratories and assorted buildings, Thomas Edison lived and worked for forty-four years, developing new inventions that have made life easier and more pleasant for millions of people.

Today the original racks of chemicals Edison used are

Chemical laboratory, Edison National Historic Site, New Jersey.

still there, just as they were four decades ago. The library remains as it was when Edison died in 1931. Even his desk is preserved precisely the way he used it last.

And in the workshop, where lathes and jigs and tools of invention now are silent, one can almost feel the presence of his genius. A placard that he posted prominently is still there. It is a quotation from the English portrait painter, Sir Joshua Reynolds, and reads:

> "There is no expedient to which a
> man will not resort to avoid the real
> labor of thinking."

Thus across the land—from Fort Sumter in South Carolina to Fort Laramie, Wyoming, to Fort Clatsop on the Oregon coast—the history of the United States is preserved in living and vivid fashion—and the people who guard this heritage can feel a special pride in their daily work.

Recreation resources are also preserved and made available for use, especially in the national seashores and national recreation areas. In these the opportunity for service to people is tremendous. Not only that, there are the added pleasures of working and playing in highly scenic locations —towering red cliffs at Lake Mead, Arizona–Nevada; subtropical seashores at Padre Island, Texas; or adjacent to historic places as on Cape Cod and Cape Hatteras.

In fact, most units of the park system are located in such a way that the ranger and his family, on days off, can readily enjoy the pleasures of hiking, swimming, fishing, camping, horseback riding and related outdoor activities.

Such, then, are the kinds of places in which the people of the National Park Service live and work. In truth, no summary can do justice to the infinite opportunities for service, or the variety of pleasant places in which that service is performed. Perhaps that is why the National Park Service— ever since Steve Mather's day—has been well-known for its *esprit de corps* and high morale.

6 · The Ranger

FOR MORE THAN five hundred years, the term "ranger" has been used to denote a person "ranging" from place to place, usually in the execution of law enforcement duties. English Royal Rangers and Texas Rangers are examples. The term "park ranger" came into use in the United States about 1901, and today the general public affixes it to virtually every person wearing the Service uniform, whether he be ranger, forester, naturalist, historian, archeologist, or superintendent.

These specialists all have definite Civil Service titles, and strictly speaking, only those who specialize in park and visitor protection can correctly be called rangers. The rest have varying titles according to the jobs they perform. To the general public, however, it is sometimes difficult to distinguish one park specialist from another. To most visitors all men in uniform are "rangers" and that's that!

The public also often confuses the park ranger with the forest ranger, and with good reason. Their jobs are similar in several respects. Each patrols and protects certain forested lands. Each helps to save human life when necessary. Each works to provide for outdoor recreation and enjoyment of wilderness and to preserve the beauty and attractiveness of the lands under his special care.

But the forest ranger is concerned far more with the commercial use of forests—cutting of timber to produce lumber and other forest products, grazing of animals, maintenance of wildlife for hunting, and the management of good forested watersheds and reservoirs for power, industry, irrigation, and domestic purposes. This means that the forests are treated partly as crops, and are managed under agricultural principles. Hence, the national forests are administered by the United States Forest Service, Department of Agriculture.

The forest ranger, therefore, studies ways and means of producing a continuous supply of commercial timber. He "cruises" through the woods marking trees for cutting or for study; he keeps a watch for harmful diseases; he examines grasslands and sees that proper grazing practices are carried out; he helps to determine game animal populations so that hunting areas and seasons can be properly fixed.

On the other hand, the park ranger is more concerned with the natural beauty of the lands he administers. The parks have been called great "outdoor museums" and the park ranger is required to preserve them in their natural state rather than to foster the production of commercial crops from them. He protects all animals equally, subject to occasional control. His forests remain uncut and unlogged in order to go through their natural cycles. Grazing, if any, is very limited, as is mining. Dams are not erected for purposes of power or irrigation. Of course, in places such as recreation areas, these policies are modified, and certain parks have laws that permit unusual practices but, in general, the ranger's job is to preserve the parks in their original condition for public inspiration and enjoyment. The National Park Service is not, therefore, an agricultural agency; it is instead a bureau of the Department of the Interior.

The uniform of the park ranger is one of his most distinguishing trademarks. It is composed of a steel gray shirt, forest green coat and trousers, and cordovan belt and shoes. The broad-brimmed hat was probably inspired years ago by that of the Royal Canadian Mounted Police. As early as

1911, a uniform of sorts was in use in the parks, and the first regular uniform was designed in 1914. After creation of the National Park Service, a committee worked on the matter and designed a uniform that was worn until 1946. At that time new changes were made and since then the same uniform, or a slight regional modification of it in some parks, has been worn by nearly all employees who meet the public.

An entirely different uniform is worn by the United States Park Police, an elite corps of highly trained law enforcement officers in and around Washington, D.C. Their responsibility is to assist visitors and maintain law and order in the parks of the nation's capital. The distinctive Park Police uniform is one of the most attractive police uniforms anywhere, and the men who wear it do so with a full measure of pride. Inasmuch as these men are highly esteemed, and their parks include such priceless shrines as the Lincoln Memorial and the Washington Monument, they have an extraordinarily high morale.

Because the parks are such prime attractions, they draw millions of visitors every year, and the basic concern of every ranger, twenty-four hours a day, is public health and safety. Each ranger must be prepared to risk his life, if necessary, to save the lives of others.

Next, the ranger is concerned with the protection of property, scenery, forests and wildlife. Each of these duties overlaps others and the job of a ranger varies widely. He must be a little of everything—gentleman, mountaineer, sportsman, daredevil, lawman, philosopher, diplomat, best pal, and all-round public servant.

His duties depend to a large extent on the nature of the park to which he is assigned. In Yellowstone, for example, winter patrols are often made on skis. In the Everglades,

In a park like the Everglades, the ranger's duties are highly varied.

Part of the ranger's time may be spent on boat patrol in the mangrove waterways, and at other times he provides assistance to boatmen, campers, and fishermen.

boat patrols lead among the picturesque islands and bird rookeries of Florida Bay. You may meet a ranger on horseback in the Sierras, or hiking in the Rockies, or swimming in the Virgin Islands. There are even ranger-pilots, who fly over the prairies of the nearly inaccessible Everglades keeping tab on wildlife, fires, and public use.

Wherever he is, the ranger must know first aid. He must be courteous. He must be understanding, because the laws he sees people breaking are likely laws they never heard of; ignorance is no excuse, of course, but the ranger is patient

and experienced enough to tell the difference between mis-
understanding and premeditated lawbreaking. He is trained
by the FBI and when he has to, he can handle the toughest
criminal. But for the greater number of park visitors, merely
being informed of an infraction is enough—for they are as
anxious to uphold the law and preserve the park as is the
ranger himself.

Protection of visitors is therefore as much a matter of
diplomacy as it is of law enforcement, and there is no place
in the National Park Service for the arrogant, brutish ranger.
Efficiency, firmness, and effectiveness characterize his actions.

Horace Albright, in his book *Oh, Ranger!*, tells the story
of a celebrity from an eastern city who was smitten with the
urge to write his name on the cone of Old Faithful geyser in
Yellowstone. It was done in a place where, as Albright relates, "The name would endure for several years before the
geyser could eliminate it by natural processes.

"This man was caught red-handed by a ranger who ar-
rested him. He was offered the choice of mixing up some
soapsuds and scrubbing the name off the cone or going
before the United States Commissioner for prosecution. He
sputtered considerably about his rights, but finally decided
to use the soapsuds . . .

"It was humiliating to have to scrub a geyser cone before
a large and not too friendly audience, and before the job
was done he was angry all through. He came to headquarters to protest about the tyranny of the rangers.

"'It's about what you'd expect from these rangers,' he
said. 'They're the dregs from the cities, out here in the
mountains because they couldn't make a living anywhere
else.'

"'Yes, I guess that's it,' said the assistant superintendent,
dryly. 'That ranger who made you wash the geyser never

had a chance. He's nothing but a grandson, and a great-grandson of two presidents of the United States.'"

Of course, as Albright goes on to say, not many rangers can claim such a distinctive background. They don't need to. It was not his distinguished forebears that made this ranger a good ranger, but his willingness to work, his devotion to duty, and his resourcefulness. The first requisite of a good ranger, says Albright, is that he be a gentleman, which hasn't anything to do with his birth or his family connections, but much to do with his manner toward his fellow men.

In the protective code of the ranger, property comes after people. This property is of two kinds—the buildings (and other public "investments" such as roads) and the park itself —its waters, forests, wildlife, and landscape.

The ranger force is equipped for immediate action in the control of fires in buildings, or if the park is within or near a city there are arrangements with local fire departments.

Protection and management of the natural features of a park are far more complex, chiefly because the natural features are lesser known. A great deal of scientific technique to do this properly is just evolving. For example, the traditional reaction to forest fires has always been immediate discovery and extinction. That still is the policy, and it is a good one. At the same time, science has found that absence of fire is changing the character of certain original forests. Long before man came, the forests were subject to repeated lightning fires, and accordingly developed in a specific way. Now such fires are quenched, and the result is that a different kind of forest is taking over.

However, eminent scientists have recommended that some fires be set in specific places and thoroughly controlled

A fire lookout peers along his firefinder to determine the direction of a distant smoke.

so that they do not burn where they are not wanted. This way the original make-up of the forest, accustomed as it was to natural fires, can be restored and preserved through selective burning.

Still, the wild, rampaging fires are fought, and it is the ranger who directs the battle. He guides the dispatching of men, equipment, and supplies. He may call for help from neighboring agencies if necessary—such as the Army and the Forest Service—or of state or local fire-fighting groups.

On the fire line, he leads fire crews in cutting a protective swath to head off the fire, in felling single burning trees called "snags," in pumping water to "hot-spots," sawing apart trees that fall across the fire line, and a hundred other jobs that finally end in "mopping-up" operations designed to make completely certain that the fire has been extinguished.

Make no mistake about it. This is a tough job, and it can be a dangerous one. The ranger plows through underbrush, claws his way across rocky slopes, and throws himself with urgency and desperation into halting the spread of the fire.

When he can go no longer and is relieved by a new shift coming on duty, he returns to the fire camp smudged with smoke, soaked with perspiration, and exhausted. He has breathed and swallowed smoke without let-up and his eyes may be vividly red and badly swollen. Yet after a few hours of sleep, he is ready for the "line" again. This can go on for days.

The last ember of a forest fire must not only be out, but cold. "Mopping up" is a dirty and laborious task.

Not all the ranger's life is spent in desperately controlling fires or enforcing laws. There are times when he feels that he is the most peaceful man on earth. On a high-country patrol to check a campsite or a lodge or an insect epidemic he tops a pass in rugged mountain terrain. It is dawn. He is alone. It is cool and quiet and restful. Before him spread majestic glacial peaks and valleys dropping away for thousands of feet.

As far as the eye can see—which may be a hundred miles —there is not a living soul apparent. At times like this he feels a certain mastery over all that is his domain. But then, from close at hand he hears the whistle of a marmot, and he knows that he is only an intruder . . . and that this is the home of the animals, which he is dedicated to preserving.

Spectacle comes to the ranger's life in other ways as well. At Hawaii Volcanoes National Park the staff may witness the sight of erupting lava fountains leaping nearly two thousand feet in the air, and of advancing red hot lava flows that go on down the mountain to smother farms and snuff out towns. Though the rangers are busy keeping curious visitors out of danger, they manage to use their cameras now and then—and they have a ringside seat.

Sometimes the ranger is about the only person left to view the wonders of nature on the rampage. When Hurricane Donna swept through Everglades National Park in 1960, it blew down trees, shattered windows, blew out screens, ripped up roofs, destroyed house trailers, swept away houses, crushed birds, and washed boats inland. Everyone was evacuated except several caretakers and the area ranger at Flamingo. At the height of the storm, with radio contact gone, glass crashing, and the wind screaming by at more than one hundred miles per hour, the ranger clung to his post in the first aid room. He expected at any moment that

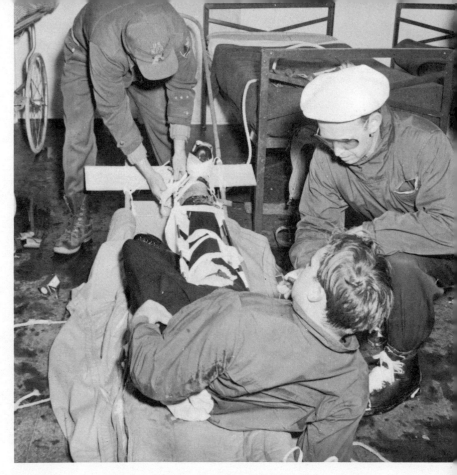

A ranger ties a leg splint while rendering first aid to a ski accident victim.

the walls of the visitor center would be caved in and the whole building washed away. But the building held, and so did the ranger. There is no better way to be first on the scene after such an event. Like the captain of a ship, the ranger stays with his park—sink or swim.

Obviously, all this means that the ranger must be in prime physical condition, able to withstand severe exposure to the elements, hot or cold, wet or dry, and long periods of sustained activity.

And there are times when he must have nerves of steel. Public safety means many things. It means the search for lost persons, using radio, aircraft, psychology, dogs—every old and new technique. It means rescue of trapped or injured persons—by rope, by stretcher, by helicopter, or by any method at his disposal. It means teamwork, and every man on the team has to be alert and observant. Each must be courageous, too, and there are cases galore of heroic rescue, most of which go unheralded because the rangers regard such things as merely part of the day's work. However, a citation of valor given to a team of rangers in Yosemite National Park shows how far beyond the call of duty a team can go:

"On the evening of August 19, 1958, a 17-year-old youth became stranded on about a one-foot-square surface in a vertical crack on an almost sheer cliff face 1,500 feet above the floor of Yosemite Valley.

"A rescue team of nine Park Rangers tried throughout the night to reach the youth from below, but were impeded by darkness and the sheer cliffs. One of them operated a bull horn to keep the boy awake so that he would not fall from his precarious perch.

"At daybreak, rescue operations were started from above. By employing the technique of rappelling down hundreds of feet of sheer rock, three members of the team, at extreme hazard to themselves, succeeded in reaching the boy by mid-morning and getting him to a big ledge. A block and tackle was set up, loose rocks were moved or stabilized, and other safety devices were rigged for the final three-hour haul to safety.

Mountain rescue is a specialized art requiring a high degree of skill and judgment.

"Although these men were trained in mountain rescue operations, this particular one far exceeded demands of the usual type in that it was accomplished only through the calculated exposure of their lives and safety. It required a superb demonstration of the most skilled techniques of rock climbing and mountain rescue practices. Its success attested to the sound training and personal courage of each member of the team, ·and to their unselfish disregard of personal risk to save the life of a park visitor.

"As a fitting tribute to an outstanding performance of skill and bravery, the Yosemite National Park Mountain Rescue Team is granted the Department's Unit Award for Excellence of Service."

Mountain rescue is not demanded of every ranger. Indeed, it is a skill entrusted to only a few who are especially trained and qualified. But the primary attribute of rescue work—dependability—is required of all. And it is required for the less dramatic tasks of writing reports and keeping daily logs, or taking care of tools and equipment. Rangers collecting fees at entrance stations, visitor centers, caves, historic houses and the like must keep a close account of their funds. After an auto accident, report forms must be accurately completed, distributed wherever required, and copies properly filed for future reference. A summary of special happenings, accidents, famous visitors, complaints— anything out of the ordinary—is usually reported in writing to the district ranger and he in turn summarizes such happenings in his district and so informs the chief ranger, who in turn may notify the superintendent. This may seem at first to be cumbersome, but the ranger soon discovers that it is all part of a day's work and becomes almost automatic. Besides, it is worth the price of reporting on paper and attending staff meetings to have a well-informed organization whose members know what is going on in the park.

Alertness and bravery are other qualities a ranger must possess. Cleanliness is a must, and friendliness, too, if he is to handle complaints from the public.

Of all his attributes, the one that comes most naturally is his love of the great outdoors. He knows his way around in it, knows how to read maps and compasses not only to find his own way when searching or rescuing but to direct visitors accurately when they want to hike to a remote canyon or climb a distant peak. He must recognize weather signs so as to warn unwary visitors of impending trouble. This is especially true in coastal parks, but there are other examples. Rangers in Yosemite have to watch for "Mono winds," which under certain atmospheric conditions, whistle through Yosemite Valley with sufficient force to uproot trees.

The ranger knows the names and uses of plants, and early in his career learns how to survive in the wilderness. It is a good thing, too, because from time to time he finds himself responsible not only for his own safety but for that of thousands of others. During an earthquake near Yellowstone National Park in 1959, roads cracked, rocks fell, landslides roared, and geyser pools exploded. Even though, at that moment, there were eighteen thousand people in the park, no panic occurred, thanks to the cool-headed rangers. Because of constant patrols and careful traffic management there were no injuries as people traveled in and out of danger zones.

Call it equanimity, if you wish, or imperturbability. There is a great deal in the ranger's life that cannot be defined or entered into the written description of his job—or in the requirements which newcomers must meet to become park rangers.

Generally speaking, a person must be twenty-one years of age or over, and must have had four years of college education, or three years of experience, or enough of both to satisfy the requirement. If he has a college degree, so much the better.

But what in? This is a good question for the graduating high school senior or the college student preparing for a Civil Service career in the national parks. Rangers may be qualified in one of several fields, as follows:

Biology	Nature Education
Botany	Nature Recreation
Conservation	Physical Geography
Ecology	Wildlife Management
Entomology	Wildlife and Resource Conservation
Forestry	Zoology
Geology	

The student decides which one or two of these he wishes to pursue, and then buckles down to work and works hard. He must never forget that ranger positions are highly competitive, and if he is going to succeed he must surpass a great many other applicants. He should also remember that the ranger's job is not primarily a job of research. This means that the field or practical aspects of college courses should be emphasized rather than strictly laboratory studies such as embryology, histology, and cytology, or non-related fields such as mining engineering.

Studies in other skills, and in the humanities, are also important since the ranger will deal so often with people. He should by all means have an excellent command of English, and should be able to speak and write effectively. He should master other courses, too, among them psychology, law enforcement, American history, introductory sociology, physical geography, fundamentals of economics, business administration, landscape design, soil conservation, drafting, and foreign languages (chiefly Spanish and French).

Certain schools and colleges of forestry, or universities with departments of natural resources, have established courses in park management for the specific purpose of preparing students to enter park careers. Rangers need not necessarily be professional foresters, but such schools come closest to providing all the recommended courses. And the more field work the student can obtain, the better his preparation for duties he will later be expected to perform. When finally he enters the National Park Service, there are additional training opportunities available, as described in Chapter 10.

Conditions change from time to time, and it is always wise to get the latest information from a nearby park, or from the National Park Service in Washington, D.C. A good way to acquire experience is to secure a summer appointment as a seasonal ranger—which is described in Chapter 10.

If Nathaniel Langford in the 1870's had had in Yellowstone the kind of rangers that are there today, his job would have been much easier. And if he were here today, very likely he would have a word for the American public: Don't worry—your parks are safe.

7 · The Naturalist

THOSE UNIFORMED EMPLOYEES who are trained in the natural sciences and who devote a great deal of time to public talks, photography, research and the like are called park naturalists. They are, in fact, men with two lives—a personal scientific one, and a public interpretive one.

Even though visitors still refer to them as "rangers" they are naturalists by virtue of their specific education and training, and the more of these, the better. A college degree is highly desirable, and if the naturalist has a Master's or Ph.D. degree, and is competent in his field, he is more likely to command a wide respect in the parks and in the scientific world. He may take a general science course in college, or may specialize in subjects such as botany, the study of plants; zoology, the study of living animals; geology, the science of the earth; ecology, the relationship of living things to their environment and to each other; forestry, and certain other courses that also qualify the ranger for appointment.

The naturalist is keenly in need of writing and public speaking skills because he so often meets the public. By the same token he needs training in psychology, history, and sociology. Drafting helps because he often prepares signs and maps for booklets or exhibits. Typing and shorthand are useful so that he can do research and prepare reports rapidly and neatly. Courses in business administration help in running his sometimes complicated office.

Though he is skilled in one endeavor, he has to have an interest and knowledge in others. A naturalist who has studied rocks and minerals closely has to know what birds

Measuring the advance or recession of glaciers sometimes calls for crossing hazardous snowfields.

inhabit his park because of questions that may arise about them.

As to that private scientific life of the naturalist—it is full of challenge and excitement. Above all else he must equip himself as an expert on the natural history of the park. To do this he explores the park from end to end. This means high-mountain hikes, boat or canoe trips, photo expeditions, and a full examination of the mammals, birds, plants, rocks, and special features of the park. He has to learn about the discovery and exploration of the region, the prehistoric Indians who once inhabited it, and what is happening to the wilderness today. All this gives him facts he needs and adds to the store of adventures that can be related to campers around a campfire.

He can tell about the time he discovered a rare and magnificent mineral in a remote canyon and how this solved some geologic riddles. He can tell about an expedition he led to photograph a natural sandstone bridge that had been seen only from the air. He can relate his adventures in studying the life history of the white-tailed squirrel, or of an encounter with a grizzly, or a search for the pink rattlesnake.

He knows where the fishing is good and where it is not. He can tell you what time of day you should go to this scenic point or that to take pictures. From the sketchiest description, he can name the flower you saw along the road, or the animal that skittered out of sight through the trees. He can name the trees in winter, when they have no leaves or flowers to help identify them, or can tell what tree a handful of mysterious seeds came from. And if there is some information he doesn't have at the moment, he knows where to find it.

Within the national park system, special projects are continually under way. Sometimes a group of naturalists will strap their food, sleeping bags, notebooks, and other equipment to their backs and trudge off into the wilderness high country to measure the advance or recession of glaciers. Work of this kind is normally accomplished in autumn, when visitors to the park are not so numerous, when skies are clear and the air is chill, and before the higher passes have been blocked by winter snows.

In the never-ending search for uncommon kinds of life, naturalists sometimes discover species new to science, particularly among the insects. Rarer kinds of living things are especially watched over, such as the calypso orchid, the black-footed ferret, the flamingo, and the American crocodile.

Naturalists go into action quickly when nature goes on a rampage. During the earthquake in the vicinity of Yellowstone National Park, rock slides and extensive cracking occurred within the park, and the geyser basins were altered in various ways. New crevices opened and steam began erupting from them. Colorful boiling mud pots burst wide open. Some geysers exploded, some got hot, some cooled off, some even quit.

As soon as the earthquake struck, naturalists went straight to the zone of shock and began recording observations—the movements of the land, the rates of eruption of the geysers,

A technician at Dinosaur National Monument chips away the surrounding rock so that a fossil bone will stand out in bold relief.

the locations of new steam vents and hundreds of other changes that had to be recorded at once.

The naturalist is wise enough to respect the hazards of the wilderness, especially when conducting visitors on tours. He does not fear these hazards; rather, he seeks to understand them. He knows where the dangerous hot springs are. He knows that deer and bear and other animals are unpredictable, and acts accordingly. Wherever it occurs, danger is taken in stride. That adds to the spice of outdoor life.

Naturalists at Hawaii Volcanoes National Park may be required to assist in the gathering of molten lava during the eruption of volcanoes. Naturalists in cavern parks occasionally prowl into little known caves to study the dripstone formations and subterranean animals, and in the process they must scramble across dangerous crevices and work their way through unknown passages.

To an outsider, the life of a naturalist seems to be exceptionally glamorous and exciting, and although some of the things the naturalist does inevitably become routine, he does have a variety of fascinating jobs and a major responsibility in the management of the park.

From time to time he lends a hand to the protective force in matters such as first aid, law enforcement, and fire control. He writes reports and letters, and reviews the content of articles, books and pamphlets scheduled to be printed. He advises the superintendent on insect infestations, animal diseases, and the nature of the forests and grasslands at the time the region was rediscovered by white men. Very often he works in close cooperation with park foresters and park biologists, and with scientists of nearby universities.

This, then, is more or less the private life of the naturalist. His public life is different. When called upon to explain to visitors the scientific things he has learned, he actually "interprets" the unfamiliar language of science so that the layman can understand. In this sense he is a real interpreter, and ever since those "nature guide" experiments in the 1920's, interpreters have become front-line troops in the dissemination of knowledge and understanding.

Naturalists are not the only interpreters, of course. There are also historians, and archeologists. On occasion, rangers, superintendents, and others on the staff may engage in interpretive programs to explain the meanings of park features and processes, or to tell about their own experiences.

When he becomes an interpreter, the park naturalist is less concerned with the acquisition of knowledge then with the delivery of it. One is impossible without the other, however. Every fact in a public talk must be checked and double checked. The public regards a naturalist as a walking encyclopedia, and considers his statements absolutely true. Few public servants have such built-in trust when they don uniforms, and so the naturalist considers accuracy an initial order of business.

Having checked his facts and interpretations, the naturalist is ready to go before his admiring audiences. This he does by giving talks at observation points, museums, lodges, campfire circles, and nearby cities. He leads the people on nature walks, flower hikes, boat tours, cave trips, ski tours, or jungle prowls.

It stands to reason that he has to speak effectively and have a good command of English. He has to think on his feet and be prepared for sudden interruptions. While he is giving a talk on park geology a bear may walk onto the stage beside him. When this happens, he changes his remarks from geology to bears—fast. The adventures of those in the service who deal with people would fill a book in

Describing the life and times of a baby possum.

itself, and are more fully discussed later on in Chapter 11.

An important part of the naturalist's public life is working with young people, and he now and then finds himself conducting classes, craft workshops, junior ranger programs, and outdoor leadership courses.

If there is a radio or television station nearby, he may frequently be called upon to speak or to work on broadcast scripts. He constructs exhibits for fairs or other special events. And whenever he can possibly find some extra minutes, he may prepare an article for publication or even write a book.

Each summer, the staffs of the parks are swelled by seasonal ranger-naturalists whose duties are primarily the interpretation of natural phenomena. These people usually work for two or three months only, dispensing information, giving interpretive talks, doing research, photographing, and engaging in much of the full-time naturalist's work. They must have had at least two years of experience in interpreting natural history, or two and a half years' study successfully completed above the high school level, with major courses in geology, or in the sciences dealing with plant and animal life in its natural state.

As it happens, seasonal naturalists come from many walks of life: teachers, scientists, college professors, foresters, students, and public speakers, to name a few. Women are by no means excluded, and they serve splendidly in nearly all the duties that fall to naturalists, historians, and archeologists. Altogether, the seasonal staff performs a "yeoman job" of summer service to travelers.

The rewards of such a profession are many—and the main one is simply knowing that the work has been appreciated. Once in a while the naturalist gets a letter like this:

"Dear Sir: From the bottom of our hearts we thank you and your staff for showing us such a wonderful time during our vacation. You ranger-naturalists made the national parks our best vacation by far. Your talks, your tours, your guided walks, your willingness to share your knowledge, your enthusiasm for the park—'our park' now—all helped to make our stay an ideal one.

"Your trails will call us back again and again. You helped us to discover an entire new world."

8 · The Historian

"CHARGE!"

The British general, resplendent in uniform and wheeling on his horse, rallied his troops and galloped fearlessly toward the American rampart.

"Charge!"

The Americans opened fire. Whatever these Kentucky and Tennessee frontiersmen lacked in military training they made up in deadly aim. The British general fell, mortally wounded, and across the battlefield, vicious holes were torn in the enemy ranks. So accurate was the American fire that the British were killed in droves.

Lead flew everywhere, beneath a pall of acrid, stinging powder smoke. Confusion turned into terror for the hapless British, and terror into panic. They fell back.

By the time the battle was over, the well-trained, well-disciplined, outnumbering British had experienced a disastrous defeat. When the casualties were counted, the British had lost two thousand men, and the Americans thirteen.

Thus went the battle of New Orleans, January 8, 1815, the site of which is now preserved as Chalmette National Historical Park, Louisiana. And such is the kind of story that the United States park historian has to tell. He searches into the past, recreates and explains great events, and makes historic times come alive with excitement as if they happened only yesterday.

Better than anyone else, the historian can agree with Cicero, the Roman statesman, that not to know what has gone on in the past is to remain always in the infancy of knowledge.

In the United States, more than 125 sites of outstanding historic importance have been set aside in the national park system, and in nearly every other park or monument there is important evidence of the lives and times of the past.

The coming of the first Englishmen to America is commemorated at Fort Raleigh in North Carolina and Jamestown in Virginia. Explorations by the Spanish are preserved in sites such as De Soto National Memorial in Florida, Coronado in Arizona, and Cabrillo in California.

A nation's freedom is sometimes forged on fields of battle, and in the United States nearly all the major battlefields are preserved as parks. Among those relating to the American Revolution are Minute Man, Saratoga, Kings Mountain, and Yorktown.

Commodore Perry's victory on Lake Erie is commemorated for all time. The great battles of the Civil War left hallowed ground to serve as reminders of the past and lessons for the future. We can relive Pickett's charge on the quiet grounds of Gettysburg today, or stroll along the silent battleground at Antietam, where more than twenty-three thousand soldiers were killed or wounded a century ago.

Great buildings of history still retain their original character, the greatest being Independence Hall and environs, where the First Continental Congress met, where the Declaration of Independence was adopted, where the Constitution of 1787 was drafted—in short, the birthplace of the United States. The Liberty Bell is still there and though it now is silent, its message rings in the hearts of freedom-loving peoples everywhere. This whole complex, in the heart of Philadelphia, is saved in perpetuity as a National Historical Park—and park historians are charged with the great responsibility of helping to keep that early story alive.

When men of the east rode west—settling a new frontier—they passed historic gateways such as Cumberland Gap and Scotts Bluff. They built and left behind such forts as Union, Laramie, and Vancouver, all preserved forever now in the national park system.

In addition to famous places there are areas dedicated to

A park historian describes the Liberty Bell.

famous men—Theodore Roosevelt National Memorial Park, Abraham Lincoln's Birthplace, and the like—and shrines of tribute to the progress of a nation: the flying field where Wilbur and Orville Wright first brought about sustained power flight, or the birthplace and boyhood home of George Washington Carver, the brilliant Negro scientist who did so much to improve techniques of agriculture.

All this is the eminent domain of the park historian, and nearly all the historic sites and parks have official park historians on duty. (Natural parks with historic values are assisted by historians from regional Park Service offices.) The park historian is a man (women are eligible, too) who has a college degree in history, or who has both education and experience that is the equivalent of a four-year college course. Once past the Civil Service entrance exams, and once through the probationary year in his first assignment, he is assured of a future that is as wide as the mind of man.

As a park historian (again, the visiting public, recognizing his uniform, may refer to him as a ranger) his first allegiance is to the people he serves—their safety, comfort, and knowledge gained during a brief stay in the park. His second allegiance is to the things he is charged with preserving—which includes the story of what happened there. He has to be sure that old historic buildings and objects do not deteriorate more than they already have. An iron halberd, used by the Spanish in Florida centuries ago, has to be chemically treated if it is not to rust away completely. Nails and bottles, buttons, glass, diaries and all the accoutrements of bygone civilization are kept and catalogued by him. Famous paintings and tapestries must be cleaned and restored from time to time, and if the historian himself does not know how to do these things, there are specialists in the Service who can. In a sense, therefore, the historian is responsible for protecting life and property just as rangers do in other parks.

The importance of the historian's job can be measured by the importance of some of the national treasures he keeps. At Independence Hall, in addition to the Liberty Bell, is the original inkwell into which our forefathers dipped their pens to sign the Declaration of Independence. Moreover, there is a fabulous collection of early American paintings by the famous artist Charles Willson Peale.

The historian watches over masterpieces of sculpture, all the way up to the size of Mount Rushmore in South Dakota, or the Statue of Liberty in New York harbor. At Gettysburg, historians keep a watchful eye on the giant cyclorama, a circular painting that takes an entire building to house. Or in Scotts Bluff National Monument in Nebraska, there is a collection of original water colors by the pioneer artist-photographer, William Henry Jackson.

Important as museum collections are, the historian has to go to extended lengths sometimes to verify the authenticity of what he acquires. This, plus the continuing need to tell an accurate story to the public through talks and walks and books, requires constant research.

To some historians, research is the most exciting part of the job. Much of what a historian seeks is elusive and most of the problems he tries to solve have all the elements of a detective story. Many a historian can cite adventures he has had in chasing down some fact or object hidden for years.

Park historians have only within the last few years discovered what the original Fort McHenry looked like. In Alaska, they have found the exact location of a fort where the Sitka Indians made their last heroic stand against the Russians in 1804. In cooperation with archeologists they uncovered the remains of "Redoubt Number Ten" on

Yorktown Battlefield, where General Washington received and signed the articles of British surrender from General Cornwallis.

Since the early history of the United States had its origins in other lands, a number of park historians have searched in foreign archives for the answers to many problems. Historians have traveled to Denmark, Sweden, England, France, Spain, and other places in the constant quest for truth.

They have interviewed famous people, particularly the descendants of men whose memory lies enshrined in the great historic places of the nation. They have also talked with pioneers—shoemakers, sailors, cowboys, Indians, explorers, and ordinary citizens.

All this has made the park historian a highly respected member of his profession, and like the naturalist, the public trusts his word. That makes the burden greater. He must be entirely accurate in what he says and writes, and this isn't always easy.

If he has sufficient facts and figures, the historian can reconstruct original rooms, or houses, or forts to look the way they did in their heyday. This is being done on a substantial scale at Fort Laramie National Monument in Wyoming and to a lesser extent at other historic sites.

The historian can create old mountain farms and industries, as on the Blue Ridge Parkway, and even hire people to perform activities that are either forgotten or rarely seen today. Examples of these are flour grinding and sorghum making of the southern highlands, canal barge trips on the Chesapeake and Ohio Canal, glassmaking at Jamestown, and even dogsled demonstrations in Alaska.

Still, the widest service performed by park historians is simply explaining to visitors the happenings that took place in these important sites, and describing the buildings,

Part of a pioneer farmstead preserved in Great Smoky Mountains National Park.

objects, stories that remain today. Like other interpreters, he delivers talks, conducts tours, writes books and booklets, and helps to create museum exhibits and audiovisual programs in a dynamic, dramatic, and effective way. Such jobs require imagination and many kinds of skill.

Places where history is being made today may eventually be established as national historic sites—Cape Canaveral is an example—and historic trails may some day be given more regard.

To the historian, many questions remain to be answered.

Historians of the future will doubtless discover hidden facts and remains in the archives of this and other nations, and in the old historic houses, forts, and battlefields that still remain.

They are also involved in related programs, of which the Registry of National Historic Landmarks is one of the most challenging. A registered National Historic Landmark is a site or building (including the homes or works of prehistoric Indians) possessing exceptional value in commemorating or illustrating the history of the United States. A survey of such sites several years ago revealed hundreds that were still in reasonably good condition and others that were deteriorating rapidly or were in danger of being destroyed to make room for modern construction.

Some landmarks were already in the national park system, but it was obvious that for financial reasons alone the Federal Government could not acquire them all. So a program of cooperation was devised whereby the Federal Government would cooperate with state and local governments and with private owners in recognizing the importance of these historic places and taking steps to preserve them. Accordingly, park historians and archeologists conducted a nationwide survey and listed the sites that were important enough to be eligible for landmark status. Each site was then approved by the Secretary of the Interior.

To register a landmark, the owner simply applies to the National Park Service for a certificate and bronze plaque, and in so doing agrees to maintain the historical integrity of the property, use it for purposes consistent with its original character, and to permit occasional visits by Park Service specialists. This is all voluntary on the part of the owners, but so far more than 550 sites have been registered. Among those eligible or registered are such well-known places as

Mount Vernon, the Bartram House and Gardens in Philadelphia, the Pribilof Fur Seal Rookeries in Alaska, Tomb-
stone, Fort Bowie, and Apache Pass in Arizona, Sutter's
Fort, Jack London's Ranch, and John Muir's home in California, and the home of Abraham Lincoln in Springfield,
Illinois. The program is administered by National Park Service historians and archeologists, and a similar registry is in
progress to recognize national scenic and scientific landmarks, a program administered by Service naturalists.

Cicero was right. To be oblivious to what has passed is to
lose our very identity, and to endanger our heritage. The
park historian knows that all too well. He knows what this
heritage means to his fellow citizens and to neighborly
nations around the world. He knows that he safeguards the
nation's character—past, present, and future. His job is to
keep the foundations of that character alive for the inspiration of young and old, now and forever.

His motto might well take the form of a question asked
by a modern historian: how do we know it's us—without
our past?

9 · The Archeologist

HE DIGS FOR HOURS in broiling sun and swirling dust. To every broken jar or mug or bowl of a bygone age he gives the tenderest loving care. He handles ancient bones as though they were more fragile than eggs, which sometimes they are.

His tools are picks and shovels, brushes, compasses, trowels, cameras, notebooks, pencils, and sacks—endless numbers of sacks in which to place his specimens for later study.

"Later" is in the laboratory, where he labels pottery, sorts out arrow points, and runs a multitude of tests on spearheads, corncobs, feathers, and cloth—the refuse of a different world and a different people. And when he has mastered his subject well, he rises before an audience and relates the story of the first Americans—one of the most fascinating subjects on earth.

To the park archeologist, the dust of centuries and the crumbling homes of early man reveal the lives and times of people long ago. How long ago is still a matter of question. The earliest people probably came to North America from Asia more than ten thousand years ago, and as time went on the generations that followed spread to the southern tip of South America. These early Indians wandered and hunted at first, then some tribes learned to farm, then settled—which gave them time to think, to build cliff cities, and to fashion pottery, jewelry, and weapons.

Today, more than twenty units of the national park sys-

A park archeologist, with broom and trowel, carefully excavates an ancient Indian pit house.

tem exist primarily because of the importance of their archeological remains. A large and spectacular concentration of sites is in the southwestern states of Arizona, New Mexico, and Colorado. These vary from single fortresses like Tuzigoot to cities such as those in Chaco Canyon and at Mesa Verde. Along the upper Mississippi River is another kind of Indian remains; at Effigy Mounds National Monument, in Iowa, occur large burial mounds in the shapes of cones or rectangles or birds and mammals. The great Mound City, near Chillicothe, Ohio, was not a city at all but a necropolis—a burial center probably for chieftains of high importance.

In general, these are national monuments of relatively small size, with only a single archeologist on the permanent staff. In the season of heavy travel, of course, other archeologists may be added on a temporary basis in order to serve a larger number of visitors.

Of the remaining 190 units of the national park system, practically all contain some evidence of prehistoric man. Grand Canyon National Park, for example, was established primarily to preserve its geologic wonders—but there are hundreds of cliff dwellings, pueblo ruins, or smaller sites within the boundaries of the park, and they are given as careful protection as any of the natural features; there is even a wayside museum of archeology that tells the story of early man in the canyon region.

Everglades National Park is a great sanctuary for birds and other wildlife, but there are also great shell mounds deposited many years ago by Indians living in the heart of the glades. Isle Royale National Park possesses prehistoric copper mines. There are kitchen middens at Carlsbad Caverns and outstanding rock drawings at the Petrified Forest.

Thus the abundant evidence of ancient man in the United States is well preserved and well interpreted throughout the national park system. And it is this extent and diversity of priceless antiquities over which the park archeologist has jurisdiction and that he is sworn to preserve.

Just like the ranger, the naturalist, and the historian, he is a full-fledged employee of the National Park Service and as such is subject to the standard opportunities of transfer from park to park. Ordinarily, he will transfer only among the archeological parks and monuments, but as his interests and experience broaden he may move into administrative posts in other types of parks, or to regional offices or even to the Washington office. Much the same is true for the park historian, from whom the archeologist differs only in that he deals with prehistoric sites (generally those sites occupied prior to the discovery of America by Columbus) and the historian deals with historic sites (dating from the time of Columbus down to the present).

When he is on public duty, the archeologist wears the same familiar uniform that rangers, naturalists, and historians do, and even though his official title is park archeologist, the public frequently refers to him by that time-honored term of "ranger."

Of course, practically speaking, the archeologist must sometimes be a combination ranger, naturalist, and historian, too, especially if his is a lonely outpost and there is no one else around. This means that while archeology is his chosen career he must also have a genuine interest in other aspects of park work, and he must know something of the birds, plants, rocks, and other objects that visitors may ask him about. He must protect human life and preserve the natural, historic, and prehistoric features of the park. And in this he has the full authority of law.

His duty to preservation stems in considerable part from the Antiquities Act of 1906, which makes explicitly clear that it is a Federal offense to remove, damage, or destroy "any historic or prehistoric ruin or monument, or any object of antiquity" situated on Federal lands. That makes looting unlawful—and prohibits even the taking of an arrow point or piece of pottery or fossil track.

Keeping the ruins safe from vandals is one thing. Keeping them safe from weather is another. This calls for the ruins to be stabilized, that is, strengthened with steel and concrete in a hidden way so that the ruins appear unchanged. Under ruins stabilization programs administered by Service archeologists, the natural erosion or crumbling of these priceless dwellings is halted, and it is a good thing. The supply of ancient ruins is definitely limited.

In certain cases, however, the march of civilization condemns some Indian sites to be destroyed forever—as during the digging of ditches for oil pipelines, or under the waters of a reservoir. Highway construction and urban expansion also take their toll. In these places the prehistoric sites must be examined once and for all.

Before pipe trenches are cut or lands are flooded, as much archeological evidence as possible has to be salvaged—which means that much of it may be unearthed and taken where it can be recorded and studied.

This procedure is known as "salvage archeology," and Park Service archeologists cooperate closely with the Smithsonian Institution and state agencies to survey threatened lands and find the ancient sites upon them. The National Park Service is responsible for recovery of early remains at all reservoir sites and along all pipelines and similar projects. It is a far-reaching job that will not end until the last dam is built or pipeline laid.

Another aspect of the park archeologist's work is that of deducing the historic past by methods usually reserved for digging up the prehistoric past. This means that certain excavation techniques can help in finding the foundations of forts or houses. This is known as "historical archeology" and it has led to a number of extraordinary new discoveries in the units of the national park system.

Archeologists found the exact location and size of George Washington's Fort Necessity, in Pennsylvania, built during the French and Indian War more than two hundred years ago. They unearthed clues to life in historic Jamestown, the earliest permanent English settlement in Colonial Virginia. They located trenches used in the Battle of the Little Bighorn, where Custer and his men were killed.

At Fort McHenry, Maryland, they found the wooden base of the flagpole from which the American flag was flying when seen by Francis Scott Key during the British bombing of Baltimore in 1814. That same day, Key wrote "The Star Spangled Banner." A replica of the historic flag still flies at Fort McHenry—and now it flies in the right location, thanks to historical archeology.

Yet for all the glamour, the park archeologist is a working man—and often his work is hard, prolonged, and dirty. He endures long hours of heat and desiccation if he digs in the desert sun. He battles swarms of buzzing mosquitoes in swampy sites, or chokes in clouds of dust churned up during excavation in caves or cliffbound dwellings. Hours in the lab, identifying and classifying pottery fragments, and then preparing a detailed manuscript recording his discoveries, requires patience and perseverance.

Behind all this lies the nagging frustration of mysteries that may never be solved at all, that his work is merely a part of a continuing process that never ends. For that matter,

In 1958, park archeologists discovered these historic, hand-hewn oak timbers seven feet deep in mud at Fort McHenry. The timbers supported a flagstaff from which flew "the star spangled banner" on that eventful night in 1814 when Francis Scott Key wrote the National Anthem.

A replica of the famous flag and pole on their original site at Fort McHenry.

Cliff Palace, in Mesa Verde National Park, may once have sheltered more than four hundred Indians.

the search for knowledge itself never ends. If the would-be park archeologist understands that the job is a difficult one, requiring stamina and stability, and if he can meet the qualifications—then he is in for one of the most rewarding of all careers.

The qualifications for becoming a park archeologist include a four-year college course, with twenty or more semester hours of anthropology—the science of man, a course in American archeology, and three months of experience in archeological excavations under the direction of a professional archeologist. Experience may be substituted for some of the college work, but the total combination must be equivalent to a four-year college course.

Seasonal positions are available during the summer and the profession of archeology is by no means limited to men. Women serve admirably as park archeologists, enduring the hardships as well as anyone, and find their work replete with rewards.

As with other Service jobs, the chief reward is working with people, including the Indian peoples of today. For example, the park archeologist at Montezuma Castle once made a study of Apache Indian dances in the nearby village of Camp Verde, Arizona, and even made recordings of their singing. While the Apaches were not the people who occupied Montezuma Castle itself, they nevertheless are modern inhabitants of the same region and are interesting for that very reason. Also, visitors may see them on their travels. Therefore, it is an important secondary part of the park story to work with and study these modern Indians.

Several parks and monuments are located in or near the Navajo and Hopi Indian reservations of northern Arizona, and park officials often attend tribal meetings and ceremonies. At Pipestone National Monument, in Minnesota,

Sioux Indians still dig pipestone from the earth and fashion it into pipes and other objects of interest. Elsewhere, local Indians present demonstrations of their skills at park visitor centers and campfire talks.

Like other uniformed employees, the park archeologist presents all kinds of public programs—walks, talks, guided tours, and evening programs. In Mesa Verde National Park he leads visitors through spectacular cliff dwellings that require them to go up ladders, into ancient rooms, through narrow tunnels, and down into ceremonial chambers. There is a great satisfaction in helping the park visitor understand and appreciate the ancient cultures that thrived here long before he came.

And as with public service anywhere, the park archeologist has his lighter moments. At Walnut Canyon National Monument, in northern Arizona, two ladies hurried to the edge of the canyon one morning and looked down into the abyss. Among the ledges far below, cliff dwellings had been built and abandoned more than eight hundred years before, and since lain empty and crumbling into ruin.

"My goodness, where are they?" asked one of the ladies, shading her eyes from the early morning sun.

"Where are what, ma'am?" the archeologist asked, coming up. "The ruins?"

"No," she replied. "The Indians. Are we in time? Are they up yet?"

10 · Behind the Scenes

WITH A ROAR, the flames leaped up the walls of the hallway and toward the bedroom upstairs. Smoke and fire billowed from the windows and from openings in the attic.

"All right, men," the fire chief shouted. "Go!"

With that signal, thirty red-helmeted men carrying hoses, axes, pikes, and hatchets poured into the house through doors and windows. For ten minutes a clattering pandemonium filled the house from floor to roof. Water sprayed out of the windows. Firemen emerged carrying rescued "bodies," which were dummies made to resemble the "owners" of the house.

At last the blaze was extinguished. The boiling smoke had been reduced to wisps of steam. The fire chief called his men outside and reported to the dispatcher: "All clear."

"Okay!" shouted the training supervisor. "Next crew! Light the fires again."

Such is life at the Horace M. Albright Training Center, where new uniformed personnel receive an intensive three-month indoctrination into the ways and means of managing parks.

The control of fires in buildings is one of the regular exercises. If·it happens that some park dwelling is about to be razed, the trainees take over, setting fire to the building and practicing various methods of suppression. Altogether, a class may start and extinguish fires in the house as many as thirty-five times before finally letting it go completely up in flames.

At the Training Center: exercises in photography (above) and rescue (below).

Also at the Training Center, rangers have exercises in fire control (above) and map and compass reading (below).

This is only one aspect of life at the Training Center, located at Grand Canyon National Park, Arizona. Classes, outdoor problems, and field trips take nearly every one of the ninety days and nights each session is convened.

New rangers, naturalists, archeologists and historians learn to fight all kinds of fire. They search, climb, read maps, inspect kitchens, practice with cameras and projectors, give talks, maintain budgets, supervise other employees, and in general find out how to do the hundreds of jobs they may be called upon to perform in their new careers.

Advanced training in the arts of communication is given at the Stephen T. Mather Interpretive Training and Research Center at Harpers Ferry, West Virginia. Thus training is a top priority matter in the National Park Service. Even in the parks themselves, training is regularly conducted—and in nearly all the skills.

Let it be clearly understood that uniformed employees are not by any means the only park employees. Far from it. The fact is that rangers could hardly do their job at all without the many people who work behind the scenes and help make the parks what they are today. A case in point is keeping the park as clean as possible. If maintenance crews were not alert and hard at work in their endless job, the park—for all its graceful scenery—would hardly be inspiring. Then there are landscape architects whose ingenious design of roads and structures keep them inconspicuous or in harmony with the purposes for which the park was set aside.

Altogether, dozens of occupational categories exist, and for persons who would like to work in parks in non-uniformed positions, there are places for construction specialists, warehousemen, accountants, clerks, secretaries, typists, personnel experts, and many others.

All things considered, the most important man in the park is the superintendent, although he will quickly tell you that he is not a boss but rather the captain of a team. A superintendent has to have a general knowledge of nearly every operation in the park. He gets this knowledge rising through the ranks, for over the years he may have been a ranger, or a naturalist, then a district ranger, then a planner, then a regional officer, then perhaps an assistant superintendent.

All this gives him the wide and varied background he needs in the exacting task of running a park. Most of all he has to work with people, in and out of the park, visitors, employees, and neighbors. He handles compliments—and complaints. He decides big issues and small. He helps determine the future of the park. In short, he is *it*, for every citizen in the nation depends on him to see that the park is preserved for the wisest public use. Every day he makes decisions, and trouble comes if he makes a wrong one.

Hence, the job of the park superintendent is not an easy one, nor is it simple or merely custodian-like. He wears the uniform as proudly as anyone else, and is an important leader in the social and economic life of the surrounding region. No one can underestimate the constant and crucial role he plays in safeguarding the American heritage.

Upward in the channel of command are regional offices, located at widely separated points in the United States. Each region—which contains many parks and monuments—is headed by a regional director. He and his staff are responsible for carrying out policies that are determined in Washington, and for helping the superintendents and their staffs operate their parks in the most efficient and economical way. The regional staff helps on various planning and public relations projects and so is composed of several kinds of specialists.

igh on the tower of
dependence Hall, student
rchitects take precise
easurements for the his-
orical record.

When Cape Cod was first established as a national seashore a naturalist and a landscape architect from the regional
office in Philadelphia went to the Cape and drew up a detailed map of the forests and other natural features there.
Later a regional historian went to the Cape to map the
important historic sites, including those dealing with the
landing of the Pilgrims. This was the beginning of a "master
plan" by which the superintendent and his staff would later
manage the park.

Highest in the chain of command is the Washington
office, which consists of a director, associate director, and
several assistant directors. Their staffs are composed of
specialists who help to draw up policy, and who cooperate
closely with Congress, the President, the Secretary of the
Interior, Federal, state, and international agencies, and

private citizens. Altogether, the operations of the National
Park Service are highly complex—as one would expect from
the necessity of managing more than two hundred diverse
pieces of property from Alaska to the Virgin Islands.

During the summertime, a great many opportunities arise
for public service in the parks. Such activities as the "Student
Conservation Program," fostered largely by the Garden
Club of America, and the Christian Ministry in the National
Parks, offer ways for young people to work and learn and
serve in the out-of-doors.

These are not administered by the National Park Service.
Neither are programs of park concessioners, which are private companies operating hotels, gasoline stations, souvenir
shops, transportation, and related services.

Each summer the concessioners employ drivers, guides,
cooks, waitresses, nurses, bellhops, chambermaids, clerks,
and service station attendants. Applications for these jobs
are handled by each concessioner, and not by the National
Park Service. These jobs are usually much sought after, and
application for them should be made as soon as possible
following the first of January. The same is true of summer
jobs with the National Park Service itself. Among positions
available are fire control aids and unskilled laborers, who
work on roads and trails and out in the forest on fire and
pest control projects. Applicants for these must be eighteen
years of age or over.

Seasonal uniformed people—rangers, naturalists, historians
and archeologists—must be twenty-one years of age or older.
They need to have the qualities permanent personnel have
—good sight and hearing, emotional stability, good appear-
ance, dependability, and knowledge of the outdoors or of
the general field in which they will work. Current informa-

tion on these positions can be obtained from park superintendents, or from the National Park Service in Washington,
D.C. (For mailing address of each park see list of areas
administered by the National Park Service, page 145.)

Behind the scenes are many adventures. Heavy storms
may break electric cables, bringing linemen out into the raw
and blustery elements. Every snowfall calls the snowplow
crews into action. Working in dangerous mountain passes—
with the wind howling and a blizzard driving sleet and snow
against the windshield—is not a job for the nervous.

After the floods and hurricanes have come and gone there
is oftentimes a clean-up job of enormous proportions—but
the maintenance crews are always there as soon as the storm
has gone. Their aim is to clear the debris away as soon as
possible so that the visitor can once again enjoy the park in
peace and safety.

Maintenance men repair a road washed out by hurricane and flood at
Cape Hatteras.

Road crews battle drifting sands in seashore places, as along Cape Hatteras, in North Carolina, and when a storm at sea sends giant waves crashing into shore, trouble is on the way. The sea has sometimes swept over Hatteras Island from one side to the other, taking roads, embankments, bridges and all. Recovery requires months or even years.

And so the work behind the scenes goes on. Carpenters and plumbers, typists and technicians, rangers and superintendents all form a smoothly working team. The visitor, struck with awe by the scenery, seldom notices what they do, and little realizes what it takes to run a park.

That is as it should be. People come to enjoy the park—and the staff is there to keep that possible. The staff is also there to do what Stephen T. Mather and the United States Congress ordered so long ago: to conserve the parks unimpaired for the benefit and enjoyment of future generations.

11 · Working with People

ONE MORNING on the rim of Crater Lake, in Oregon, a park naturalist stood beside an observation shelter talking with visitors as they came and went. A well-dressed man of middle age, carrying a cane, approached and asked the naturalist to tell him a little about the lake.

As nearly everyone knows, this lake—nearly six miles across and 1,932 feet deep—lies in the crater of an extinct volcano and is such a vivid and magnificent blue that hardly anyone would attempt to describe it.

As the naturalist alternately talked and listened to questions asked by the man, he suddenly and joltingly realized that the man was blind.

No sooner had he realized this than the man asked him to describe the lake.

Probably no two naturalists would have responded alike to such a challenge. This one did not hesitate. He led the blind man into the shelter, where there was a large relief model of the park. Know that a blind man's fingers were extra sensitive and that he literally "sees" through them, the naturalist placed the man's fingertips on the model and moved them from place to place as he described the scene.

He could never have described the blue of that lake—and he didn't try—but he did what he could, to the heartfelt gratitude of the visitor who would never see it.

If there is one thing a ranger learns early, it is to work with people, all kinds of people, all races, all colors, all

103

creeds. To be sure, this is not always as simple as it seems. Sometimes park visitors are tired, or angry, or surly, or even downright insulting. But experience shows that people like that are few and far between. For the most part, visitors are friendly, cheerful, interesting, and often eager to learn more about what they have come to see.

Every one of these visitors is considered "special," but now and then a world-famous person visits the park and is accorded appropriate attention. In the course of his career each ranger or interpreter or superintendent, consistent with his regular duties, may arrange for visits by kings and queens and presidents, or eminent singers, authors, dancers, and film stars.

After the home of Franklin D. Roosevelt in Hyde Park, New York, was designated a National Historic Site in 1944, the personnel who were later assigned there gathered first-hand information from the Roosevelt family and from friends. Mrs. Roosevelt consented to prepare a recorded tour of the rooms in the house. Accompanied by a historian taping her remarks on a portable recorder, she went from door to door in the mansion, telling how each room was used, and relating humorous, personal things that happened in them. The final studio recording of this conducted tour was made by Mrs. Roosevelt in 1962, the year of her death. The recording now, of course, is priceless.

Rangers conduct a considerable number of foreign dignitaries through the parks. To these people the scenic wonders and historic sites are part and parcel of the character of the United States. When a ranger, moreover, can speak their language fluently, he strongly advances the cause of international friendship and good will. In certain cases, foreign language tapes and publications are available.

By far, the greater number of visitors to every park are

less well known, and less well traveled. Their reactions to the wonders in the parks are interesting to observe. Some persons who have spent their lives on the plains have never seen a mountain before—and they take pride in telling the ranger how they felt when they first saw the mountains in his park.

This recalls what the author Charles F. Lummis said about persons who saw Grand Canyon for the first time: "I've seen people rave over it; better people struck dumb with it; even strong men who cried over it; but I have never yet seen the man or woman that expected it."

It is only natural for visitors to be confused occasionally. After all, they do not ordinarily live in a wild environment, or beside a historic shrine. One night when a ranger was giving a campfire talk to nearly five hundred people, a woman clad in pajamas wandered down the aisle and up to the stage before she realized where she was. She turned and saw in the darkness a sea of faces looking at her. "Oh, my goodness!" she exclaimed, and fled as fast as she could go.

Wherever he talks to people and helps them, the ranger repeatedly makes friends, and often these turn into lasting friendships. In the process, the ranger learns about different kinds of people from different parts of the world—their likes and dislikes, their work, their adventures, their hopes and ambitions. In return, he shares with them his own experiences and, inevitably, his special brand of conservation.

Hardly a day goes by that doesn't bring an amusing comment or question by a visitor. The great majority of visitors ask serious, sensible questions, and to the ranger there is no such thing as a "silly question." Nevertheless, the out-of-doors is such a strange environment that once in a while a visitor poses a question without realizing what he is saying. For some reason, caves promote an unusual number

A park historian tells the story of an old Spanish fort at Castillo de San Marcos National Monument, Florida.

of these. "Is this cave all underground?" "Is it darker in this cave at night?" "How many miles of this cave are undiscovered?" Or the classic comment heard on an inbound cave tour: "Looks like the farther we go down, the deeper it gets!"

Some people figure that the ranger possesses absolute control of the wonders they see. A question at Yellowstone is: "Do you keep Old Faithful running in winter?" (It runs all winter, of course, and the rangers have nothing to do with its eruption schedule; in fact, they haven't even tried to figure out how to turn it off!)

A common query comes from visitors who have driven miles from their route and upon arriving at the entrance station ask: "Is this park worth going to see?"

There is the classic tale of a visitor to Grand Canyon who

walked up to the ranger at the rim and asked: "Where's the golf course?"

"There isn't any, sir," replied the ranger.

"Well, then, when's the dance tonight?"

"There isn't any dance, either," the ranger answered.

The visitor scowled. "Well, what are we supposed to do, look at the scenery?"

In North Carolina, signs along the Blue Ridge Parkway point out that you are passing through a natural watershed, or mountain valley where rainwater collects in a reservoir that supplies the city of Asheville. Certain visitors arrive at

"Underwater trail" in the Virgin Islands is the site of naturalist-led snorkeling trips. Swimmers may also find underwater labels beside corals and other features.

Craggy Gardens still uncertain as to what a watershed is. On alighting from their car, they notice a picnic shelter on the skyline about five hundred yards away, and immediately ask the ranger: "Is that the watershed?"

All these questioners have good intentions, probably none more so than the visitor who said: "You got a wonderful park here, ranger. I hope Congress builds some more of them."

Some tales become legends, are told so often, and are so wild that one doubts the truth of them. One of these concerns the lady who many years ago, drove through miles of meadows lined with white-barked aspen trees and finally arrived at the entrance to the north rim of the Grand Canyon, in Arizona.

"My!" she said. "It's awfully nice of you rangers to whitewash those trees each year to make the forest look so pretty. What kind of trees are they?"

"Aspen trees, ma'am," replied the ranger.

"Aspirin trees?" she said in astonishment. "So that's where aspirins come from!"

"Yes, ma'am," he answered, without batting an eye, "and there's just enough iron in the soil to make the little boxes they come in."

The rangers long ago learned that the public takes these natural wonders seriously, and generally it is not good policy to joke about them; the truth is hard enough to believe. But people also appreciate good-natured humor, and the ranger who can handle it right soon has his audience in the palm of his hand.

Humorous anecdotes also come by mail. In Lake Erie, near where Commodore Oliver Perry won a decisive victory over the British in 1813, is now established Perry's Victory and International Peace Memorial National Monument. That was too long a title for one writer. The superintendent received a letter addressed to Perry's Victory International Peach Memorial.

The list of anecdotes is virtually endless. In fact, the scenic beauty of the parks, and their awesomeness and fascination, supply a continuous background for a wide range of adventure. Motion picture writers and producers certainly think so. Although production of motion pictures is restricted so that the landscape will not be damaged, a number of films have been produced in the parks or near them: *Shane* at Grand Teton; *Davy Crockett* in the Great Smoky Mountains; and *Journey to the Center of the Earth* in Carlsbad Caverns. Park rangers work in close cooperation with movie companies and once in a while hire on as "extras" during their off-duty hours.

Working with children: a park naturalist supervises the "Junior Ranger" program in Yosemite National Park.

The ranger participates in special events outside the parks: fairs, jamborees, meetings, lectures, seminars, and training programs—to name a few. He also works very closely with specialists such as researchers, mountain climbers, and photographers.

One of the most pleasant tasks is the conduct of special programs for young people. School children come in droves during the spring and fall, and in summer there are splendid opportunities to help with activities of boy and girl scouts, campfire girls, YMCA, Audubon Society, church and other groups.

Nothing keeps the ranger more on his toes than working with children. He has to be alert to their likes and dislikes and the sudden turn of their interests. Suppose he is speaking around a campfire and someone in the group asks him to lead a star walk. Up he goes—and the rest fall in behind. Atop the nearest hill he talks about stars and constellations, the moon, the Milky Way, and anything else the amateur stargazers ask about.

Or he may be asked to conduct a fern walk (pointing out all the ferns along the trail), or a moss walk, or an insect walk. He cannot be an expert in all these fields and he never tries to appear so, but he answers what questions he can and beyond that refers the group to the park museum, to a published booklet, or to a library.

Young people listen intently when a ranger tells how he fights forest fires and rescues people. They watch entranced as a naturalist handles snakes and turtles and frogs with confidence. At the same time the meaning of conservation is made completely clear, and the children get the message. All this is probably one of the greatest services that a ranger or an interpreter performs.

One night a naturalist in Prince William Forest Park, near

Washington, D.C. led a group of 120 boys on a night prowl along a forest stream. From time to time they stopped and gathered together so that the naturalist could make them aware of frogs, foxes, racoons, whip-poor-wills and other animals to be heard in the darkness.

A few days later the naturalist got a postcard in the mail. On it was a childish scrawl which read:

"Dear Ranger, I hope you are O.K. I hope your animals O.K. I hope the woods are O.K. like we left them. I hope nobody have left paper out there.

Sincerely, Ellsworth"

12 · Working with Animals

THEY KILL AND MAIM and claw and scratch—yet they are the most-loved creatures in the national park system. They chew up signs, create traffic jams, beg, steal, turn over trash cans, rip open tents, and tear up automobiles—but the public considers them absolutely adorable. They are the bears of the national parks. They are also the most dangerous beggars that ever come to a roadside.

"Cute" they may be, but they weigh five hundred pounds, and behind their vicious claws are muscles of steel and an animal brain that obeys the laws of the wild. That is one of the major reasons behind those DO NOT FEED THE ANIMALS signs. It simply is not safe. The other major reason is that animals thrive much better on a diet of natural foods—bees, worms, vegetation—than on the endless stream of cookies, marshmallows and soda pop offered by an admiring public.

One of the ranger's biggest jobs in handling animals is to keep the animals out of trouble, keep them thriving, and keep them from harming visitors. He can't do it without public help, however. The signs mean what they say.

Steve Mather laid down the policy long ago: parks are places where wild creatures are to be seen in their natural environment. Since park animals are wild, they cannot be called with a snap of the fingers . . . at least not every time they are wanted. The enterprising visitor will stalk his animals, pioneer fashion, but for his own safety he'd better know something about each creature's habits and actions

It is nap time for bruin when the ranger delivers an immobilizing drug. In fifteen minutes of slumber, the bear gets a careful medical exam.

before he follows it and sneaks up on it in the wild. This art of stalking is mastered by a few photographers, but it requires more time and patience than most people have.

Park policy also demands the conservation of *every* kind of animal—predators included. Predators—such as mountain lions, coyotes, hawks, and eagles—are not very popular in some places. Angry farmers and ranchers accuse them of doing great harm to livestock, which places the National Park Service in a difficult position. On one side the rangers are accused of breeding "varmints" that attack and kill, and on the other side are ordered to preserve all predators lest they became extinct. Each controversy is considered on its merits, but the ranger has to uphold the law—and the law says protect all animals.

The story goes that a Yellowstone ranger years ago was seen with a high-powered rifle, and a visitor asked if that was to shoot the bears when they bothered the people.

"Naw," he replied, "it's to shoot the people if they bother the bears!"

Rangers don't go that far, but they are meticulous in watching over wildlife. That is why the ranger moves a rattlesnake from some heavily visited area to a more remote spot—so that it can live its life in peace and safety as a genuine part of the natural scene. This way he quietly protects the public *and* the animal, and nary a life is lost on either side.

It is clear, therefore, that while parks are for people, they are also for animals. Even so, the ranger tries to provide as many opportunities as possible for people to witness native animals in a wild state.

Sometimes visitors nearly love the animals to death. Bird nesting areas, or rookeries, must occasionally be closed to entry during nesting time. If people come too close, the mother birds might fly away in fright and accidentally kick the young birds out of the nest. That would spell the end of the young—either by drowning if they fell in the water, or by being captured and eaten by a prowling fox. The fox gets enough to eat without this kind of help from man.

Parks are as full of fishing tales as anywhere else, from the fur-covered fish of Glacier to the mountain-climbing fish of the Yellowstone. Horace Albright tells of the Yellowstone ranger who carried a club when he went fishing. "Yeah, fishin' club," the ranger explained. "There's a big trout in there that's grabbed every fly I had but one and bit the leader in two. I take the fishin' club along to whang the big devil over the head and drive him away so I can catch some of the other fish."

Fishing—for the pure sport of it—is a favorite pastime of the ranger, and he knows where to go. Trout is the most common fish in the parks, and the abundance of them offers a delightful sport to the travel-weary angler.

The ranger is often asked why hunting is prohibited and fishing permitted in most of the national park system. The answer is rooted in law, and the law in tradition. Park wildlife is not to be harmed in any way, not even to be caged; it has been that way for decades and the law is clear. But harvest of fish is an exception. For one thing, fish are sealed off in a special restricted environment. For another, they can be caught and returned without harm, thus providing continuous sport. "Fishing for fun," as this technique is called, requires that anglers return to the water all fish within certain limits. The whole idea is to make sure that the fish are preserved for other sportsmen to enjoy.

Fish populations are managed wisely just as are all aspects of life in the park. Rangers and their research colleagues

Fishing and photography in Glacier National Park, Montana.

find out what the original condition of lakes and streams was—then restore to them the wild and native fish, if any, that once were there. Life on coral reefs and elsewhere in the offshore waters of seacoast parks is similarly managed; creatures there are allowed to live their lives in as natural a way as possible, and fishing is encouraged as long as the species there are not brought to the edge of extinction.

Sadly enough, however, some wildlife must be destroyed. When animals endanger human life repeatedly, for example, their lives must be taken. The same is true when animals increase in such numbers that they threaten to eat too heavily on park vegetation, thus starting erosion and de-

Animal life at the edge of the sea is studied and preserved at Acadia National Park in Maine.

stroying the landscape. But even in these cases, the rangers are finding ways of capturing and removing animals without having to harm them. A certain number of "exotic," or non-native, animals have entered the parks in times gone by. Examples of these are wild burros at Grand Canyon, boars in the Great Smoky Mountains, goats at Hawaii Volcanoes, and mongooses in the Virgin Islands. These creatures compete with native animals or even prey upon some of them, and since they damage the food and water supplies of scarce original wildlife they must be controlled or eliminated.

For nearly the first fifty years of its existence, the National Park Service followed a policy of wildlife *protection,* which was indeed the desperate need of Mather's day. But times and conditions change, especially outside the parks, and the time eventually came when the Service had to do more than merely protect its animals. It had to maintain a given condition in plant or animal populations, and a given habitat in which they lived. When these conditions were exceeded, measures had to be taken before the animals or the park itself were destroyed. In short, the animals and their homes had to be *managed.*

Wildlife management is not as easy as it sounds. Years ago, some Arizona cowboys proposed to drive eight thousand deer from the north rim to the south rim of Grand Canyon, but not a single deer completed the trip. The deer simply would not be driven.

The control and removal of animals is not always a pleasant task, but if the park—and the natural, normal wildlife population—is to be preserved, it is a necessary one. This job is performed exclusively by and under the direction of park rangers.

The objective of all this is to restore the primitive scene

as a vignette of early America, to maintain each park as nearly as possible in the conditions that prevailed when the area was first visited by the white man. Parks are small enough as it is, and according to eminent scientists who have studied the matter, naturalness, above all, should prevail. This is highly agreeable to the park ranger, for the protection and maintenance of the parks in their natural condition was probably one of the central challenges that led him to his career.

He must watch over animal feeding grounds as well. Nowhere is this more apparent and critical than in the Everglades of southern Florida. Thousands of animals, especially birds, live inland or on islands just off shore, but they feed on abundant fish and other forms of food throughout Florida Bay. Thus the ranger must be sure that the aquatic life upon which these creatures feed is never depleted lest the birds disappear as quickly as though they were hunted and shot.

The deer and elk of the Grand Tetons and other mountain regions often migrate outside parks and into national forests or other lands that are administered by the Forest Service, Fish and Wildlife Service, or by state agencies. It thus behooves the National Park Service to cooperate in a neighborly fashion with these agencies to assure the safety and perpetuation of the animal herds.

Wildlife management in the national parks is a never-ending job because as the "total environment" of the earth is changed by smog and pollution and the encroachments of man, the park specialists face new challenges in keeping animals in a natural state. Then, too, the patterns of animal life also change as the years go by, of which Isle Royale offers a splendid example.

Rangers on Isle Royale, in Lake Superior, are witnesses to one of the most delicate and interesting animal relation-

Rangers keep tab on some of their elk by special ear tags and neck bands.

ships in any park. There, some two dozen timber wolves, remnants or descendants of a band that came across the ice from Canada in the late 1940's, are thriving in the midst of plenty—a national park that protects them and the six hundred moose on which they feed. Decades ago there was neither wolf nor moose on Isle Royale (the moose arrived about 1912). In this newfound sharing of the island, both groups of animals have come into a balance of life. The wolves prey on old and ill as well as young, thus keeping the moose from overpopulating the island. Surviving moose are vigorous and healthful.

Finding this out is a job that calls for winter flights over the island, snowshoe trips, and periodic stays in cabins on the island. Rangers and their research colleagues, including scientists from cooperating universities, will tell you there's nothing to equal this kind of study as a way of life. Apparently neither winter studies nor summer visitors are disturbing the delicate hold that the slender population of wolves has on the island. The wolves may not exist here in large numbers, but this is the highest density of wolves found anywhere in North America. There is every reason to believe that the animal community will continue to thrive as it is. Perhaps the sorely beset timber wolf, exterminated nearly everywhere else, has found a home and some friends at last.

Science itself has not perfected the methods by which a park's original ecology—the relation of life to landscape—can be restored. But just because these things are difficult is no reason to despair of hope. Park rangers and their colleagues in special fields of research are continuing year by year to assure that the parks remain as beautiful tomorrow as they are today—and to be sure that there are always bears to chew and scratch and claw—and to be seen by their admiring public . . .

SEQUOIA BEAR THROWS A WILD FAREWELL PARTY

Sequoia National Park, California, Nov. 16, 1959. A big black bear was banished to the hinterlands today on charges of breaking and entering, auto boosting and reckless driving.

Park rangers said the bear, cold sober, turned up Saturday night for a party at the Giant Forest Lodge and:

Broke into a convertible, was chased away, returned, tore the top off the convertible, ate some food, was chased away.

Returned, converted another convertible the hard way and was chased off by the irate owner.

Returned, broke into a foreign sports car, and climbed into the driver's seat. Then, somehow, the brake released.

Off went the sports car, lickety-split, with the bear behind the wheel. The little car, tough for beginners to handle, careened down the hill and—kerash!—into a ditch.

The bear, obviously unnerved, climbed out of the wreckage, scrambled up on the roof of the lodge and—the final indignity—fell through the skylight.

Rangers found him in the kitchen amidst the shattered glass, soothing his jangled nerves with leftovers.

As an act of kindness, the rangers offered the bear a lift way, way up into the high, high Sierra, far, far from the maddening sports-car throng.

Before dropping him off, however, they painted his rump a bright red to identify him as a driver with a previous record in case he is ever picked up again for speeding or something. They said this was Park Service policy.

An official of the State Department of Motor Vehicles in Sacramento said the Park Service might have something there.

13 · Exploring New Frontiers

PEOPLE MULTIPLY and cities grow and life, it seems, becomes more hectic every year. To flee the cares of city life, more people seek the peace and quiet of the national parks. They flock to outdoor recreation areas, which become more crowded, and when that happens, other places for outdoor recreation must be found.

But this is where the trouble comes. It is the "quiet crisis" of our time. There is not much free space left. New parks must sometimes be established on property that belongs to other people, and at the first suggestion of a survey to determine whether or not the site is satisfactory, the National Park Service is attacked.

"Land grabbers!" comes the shout. "The Park Service is trying to steal our land and lock it up!"

The Service, of course, does nothing of the sort. It can't. But during the process of establishing new parks, its planners occasionally must suffer vexation in their efforts to save for all the people a little of what is left.

National parks and related areas may be created in a variety of ways. A private citizen may rouse his neighbors to the need for preserving a nearby mountain or canyon or lake or seashore. They urge their representatives in Congress to draw up and introduce a bill that would create such a park. Any proposal, however, is brought to the attention of the Secretary of the Interior, who asks his advisors and the National Park Service whether the area is worthy of being established.

Park planners go out to investigate and the first question they ask is whether an area is of national significance. If not, it might become a state park, or a county park. Then they try to find out whether the area still has integrity. Has it been ruined in some way? Are the original plants and animals still there, and if not, can they be restored? Is there enough surrounding land to offer a little buffer protection or for public access to the central features and values of the proposed area? And lastly—is it possible for the land to be purchased and set aside? If it is not public land, then who owns it? Will the owners sell? How much do they want?

For persons who do have homes on lands under study, the fears begin to rise. They may think they are going to be evicted if the land on which they live becomes a park. The battle begins. Newspapers enter on one side or the other. Public meetings and hearings are held. Some citizens rise to attack the National Park Service; others rise to defend it.

By such an exchange of opinion, every part of a proposal is examined. Ideas that provoke too much opposition may be abandoned or modified. Ideas that are difficult to understand are clarified. And the homeowners are assured that no one has any intention of removing them from their land where it is humanly possible to arrange for their remaining. Even if a park is established they are likely to have "life tenancy," which means that they can live there the rest of their lives, even after they sell their land to the Government.

Some proposals take years to succeed and some do not succeed at all. But others are recommended by the Secretary of the Interior, introduced into Congress, debated, and finally passed. The President signs the Act into law. Land is acquired. Persons are transferred in from other parks, or hired in part on a local basis. Facilities for public use and enjoyment are planned and built. At long last, the park is

dedicated, and a new unit of the national park system comes
into being.

All this is not a fixed procedure, but generally speaking, it
is the basic story of the birth of a park. As the years go by,
the boundaries may be adjusted, or if for some reason beyond control the park is damaged or loses its integrity, it
may be abolished by Congress. Meanwhile, the planners
have gone to new proposals. Once again, in response to
demand, they are at work to create recreation areas that are
population-oriented, to investigate new parks or historic
sites, or otherwise to preserve some spot of land for the
benefit and enjoyment of all the people. They have enduring
patience. They need it.

A Washington, D.C. newspaper once said: "We have
sometimes been critical, even strongly critical, of the stiff-
necked attitude of the National Park Service. When it stands
like Horatius at the bridge, blocking some project vital to
the emerging new Washington, patience runs low.

"On the other hand, if it had not been for the National
Park Service, Washington might well have lost, or perhaps
never have acquired, what amounts to one of the finest park
systems in the world."

Without the work of planners and the spirited help of the
Sierra Club, the Audubon Society, the Garden Club of
America, the Wilderness Society, and many other conservation groups, the nation would be much poorer. There might
not be any stately redwood groves, or wild rivers, or public
seashores stretching uncluttered for miles.

The fighting spirit of all these organizations can have a
telling impact. They have blocked proposals for dam construction that would have backed waters into the national
parks. They have halted highways that threatened to over-
run historic shrines or scenic sites. They have supported

additional parks to meet the demands of a growing nation. In short, they have fought for the America of the future.

Working with conservation organizations and similar groups is the pleasant side of the planner's job. Whatever he has been—a ranger, a naturalist, superintendent, or land-scape architect—he has linked his experience with that of others outside the Service. His enthusiasm has risen with theirs and when the job is over, the planner can rest secure. As with Steve Mather, there will never come an end to the good that he has done.

14 · Around the World

THE RANGER could hardly believe his eyes. He raised his binoculars again. There they were—thousands of them—a vast procession of gazelles and wildebeest and zebras moving slowly across the Serengeti Plains. Nowhere else in Africa had he seen so grand a spectacle. Riding on, he passed lions lazily lying in the sun. Away in the distance, through a shimmering haze of heat, he could make out a herd of elephants feeding. Not far away, at the base of a low ridge, giraffes were eating tender leaves in the tops of trees. A hyena wandered nervously nearby.

Back home in the United States he had never witnessed a sight to compare with this. Not in Yellowstone, or Grand Canyon, or Yosemite was there a display that could even closely match this one in Serengeti National Park, Tanzania.

Around the world, the first of all national parks—as such parks are known today—was Yellowstone. But it was not the first park to be set aside for public benefit, nor was the United States the first to set aside public parks. No one knows what country did. It is possible that the ancient Sumerians, or Babylonians, or Egyptians reserved for general use some portions of public or royal lands. So, probably, did the Greeks and Romans. In fact, the Roman lawgiver, Justinian, is said to have laid down the principle that beaches and shorelines belonged to all of the people.

In China, centuries ago, parks were created for the display

of animals. India, well before the time of Christ, declared that certain species of birds and mammals were totally protected, and established "Abbayaranya," or places "where beasts could roam about without any fear of man." Lord Gautama Buddha himself, five hundred years before Christ, preached in a deer park near Barnaras. The "Wood of the Hague," Holland, was reserved in 1576, and in 1853 the Forest of Fontainebleau, south of Paris, France, was set aside. But it remained for Yellowstone to use the term "national park" for the first time, and to set the modern example.

After Yellowstone the tradition of national parks for the enjoyment of all the people gained momentum on a worldwide scale. Canada created Banff National Park in 1887. Australia first established parks in 1891, New Zealand in 1894. Great Britain set up a national parks board; Mexico started work on its park system; and what was to become South Africa's famous 8,000-square-mile Kruger National Park was first placed under protection in 1892. Then followed Sweden, Switzerland, Russia, Italy and many others. During 1925, King Albert of Belgium created in the Congo a gorilla sanctuary that was enlarged to become the world renowned Albert National Park.

Great strides were made in the 1930's in Chile, Argentina and Ecuador. Japanese officials, after visiting the United States, began to build a system of parks and "quasi-parks" that now occupies some five per cent of the land area of the country. After World War II a number of outstanding African parks were set aside, among them Serengeti, Queen Elizabeth, Tsavo, Wankie, and Kafue.

Today more than eighty nations have established national parks and equivalent reserves, the largest single unit being Canada's Wood Buffalo National Park, 17,300 square miles—

five times the size of Yellowstone. These different park systems are administered in various ways, and by park rangers (often called wardens) whose duties and uniforms differ from country to country.

In some lands, the ranger staff is spread pretty thin. Apprehension of poachers, especially in the wilder parts of Africa, is such a problem that little time is left for the ranger to serve the park visitor. This is a matter of first things first; if the animals are lost, the visitor will have nothing to see.

One of the most dramatic adventures in saving animals and stimulating interest by native peoples in wildlife was the rescue operation performed by Rhodesian wardens when the Kariba high dam was built on the Zambesi River. Water rising behind this dam began to fill the valleys. It rose around hills and made them islands that soon were submerged entirely. Animals gathered atop these disappearing islands as a last refuge—and it was the job of the rangers to rescue them before they starved or were drowned.

Racing against the slowly rising waters, wardens and their helpers threw up nets across the islands and then spread out through the forest and drove the animals toward the nets. Gazelles, elands, kudus, baboons, and a host of other animals became ensnared, were captured and bound, loaded on canoes, and taken to the mainland to be released. They called this "Operation Noah."

Elsewhere around the world, rangers and custodians are engaged in a desperate struggle to save some of their animals from complete extinction. In Indonesia, scarcely four dozen Javan rhinos (if that many) remain alive. Their footprints are observed from time to time in the Udjung Kulon preserve, but that is about all. The animals themselves have not been seen in years.

Assistant game rangers, after driving these impala into nets, seized them, tied them, and transported them by boat to the safety of the mainland.

A senior game ranger of the Rhodesian, Africa, Game Department holds a young bushbuck doe which was rescued from an island during *Operation Noah* and later released on the mainland.

Armand Denis, the noted photographer and explorer, says that ninety per cent of the wildlife of Africa has disappeared through uncontrolled hunting and trapping—and loss of habitat—in the last fifty years.

Square-lipped rhinos very nearly disappeared from South Africa, and had it not been for strict conservation measures the animals would have gone forever. They have made a comeback, happily, and rangers are transferring them from near the Umfolozi Reserve to national parks and other sanctuaries where they will be safe. (If only some of our American forebears had created a reserve for the passenger pigeon before it was too late!)

Park rangers of other lands work under trying conditions to save what they have, and since the wildlife treasures they are striving to protect are valuable to us all, the world owes them respect and gratitude—and the help they can give.

Many species of animals are endangered, being either hunted or crowded toward extinction. Their customary ranges disregard national boundaries, and so their protection is a matter of international concern. National parks, consequently, are of worldwide significance.

That is why the United States park ranger was watching the wildlife of Serengeti National Park with such an interest. He was there to help Tanzanian authorities plan the preservation and orderly development of their parks. He was, in a way, symbolic of a hundred years of park experience which the United States has gained since Yellowstone. But this is a two-way street. The people of Africa have a long and varied experience in wildlife management. By talking to them on the spot, the United States ranger can bring to his own country extremely helpful ideas.

The United Nations itself is deeply interested in the worldwide values of parks. Under the auspices of UNESCO, the educational, scientific, and cultural arm of the UN, there was created in 1948 a new organization that has come to be known as the International Union for the Conservation of Nature, or IUCN for short. The IUCN, with headquarters in Morges, Switzerland, dedicates itself to saving wildlife and landscapes and to discussing ways of preserving natural resources. Many persons who cannot help directly, as rangers do, share in the work of the IUCN and thereby help to carry out the world conservation program.

In 1962, the United Nations passed a resolution calling on all nations to help beautify and safeguard landscapes and sites. These were considered a "powerful physical, moral

(Over) Banff National Park, Alberta, Canada. More than eighty nations have systems of national parks or equivalent reserves.

and spiritual regenerating influence, while at the same time contributing to the artistic and cultural life of peoples." Furthermore, said the report, they are important "in the economic and social life of many countries, and are largely instrumental in ensuring the health of their inhabitants."

The UN and IUCN have held many conferences around the world on parks and conservation, and have issued a voluminous descriptive listing of parks and reserves in many lands.

FAO, the food and agricultural organization of the United Nations, has a vital role in park and wildlife matters—for it is just as interested in studying the values of lands developing without the influence of man, as lands affected by human activities. Native animals in Africa, for example, have proven to be more nutritious than cattle, and far more economical to raise as food. And raising wildlife is much less destructive to the countryside.

Parks have a proven value in building good will among nations. In interchanges of park personnel there is a great exchange of ideas and friendship, and a ranger knowing other languages is extremely valuable in this kind of work.

Park rangers have gone overseas to help tell the world what the United States is like. In so doing, they have become ambassadors of good will. The purpose of such assignments is not only to attract visitors to American shores, but to show that the United States has a mature and inspiring philosophy in regard to its resources, and that all nations with a sharing of conservation knowledge can be drawn together in deep and abiding friendship.

On one such trip, two rangers toured seven nations of Europe in company with officials of other government offices and of private airline and bus companies. At sales meetings, where they met with embassy officials, industrial executives, and travel agents, they projected a series of color transparencies, and talked about the American heritage. They talked about things most likely to be appealing to Europeans —the desert, the tropics, hiking, camping, wilderness—and solitude.

"We Americans preserve our wild places undisturbed," said one, projecting a scene of the road in Death Valley. "See that road? Stop along it any time. Get out of your car and walk away a few feet or a few miles. You will be surrounded by the quiet and solitude of the wilderness. Even here in a land so often hostile, you can go away with memories that will last forever. Here are no sirens, no whistles, no cares—only beauty and peace and quiet where you can be by yourself and re-create your soul."

The effect of this on the listeners was electric, especially in Belgium and the Netherlands, where the concentration of persons per square mile is greater than anywhere else.

"I've never seen anything like it," said an Amsterdam travel agent. "We've had scenery-selling programs before, but never like this. We're always told to send our clients to New York, Chicago, Washington, Philadelphia and back. But you have shown us that the cities are also gateways, that beyond them lies another part of America, and that in it you have kept some places wild and free and dedicated to the highest of ideals."

He paused and spread his hands in amazement. "You have shown us for the first time," he said, "that America has a heart."

15 · Challenge of the Future

As sure as dawn, more parks are going to be created. There will be more parks and parkways and historic shrines, and what there will probably be most of is national seashores, lakeshores, rivers and similar recreation areas. The American people are determined to have more places to camp, to hike, to play, to swim . . . or just to be alone. And the more hectic and crowded the modern world becomes, the more valuable these places are.

Several years ago a California boy of seven hiked to some open land near his home to hunt lizards. On the way, he discovered that a baseball field and several houses were being built in a canyon where he liked to play. He turned and went to another open canyon that he knew very well, and there found tractors tearing up the land so that houses could be built.

Angered and defeated, he ran back home, took a paper and pencil and wrote a letter to the President of the United States.

"Dear Mr. President," he said, "we have no place to go when we want to go out in the canyon because there ar going to build houses. So could you set aside some land where we could play? Thank you four listenig . . ."

The President turned the letter over to Secretary of the Interior, Stewart Udall, who replied to the boy that he was very much aware of the need to be able to hunt lizards and follow ants and just lie on one's back and watch the changing shapes of the clouds . . . all alone. The Secretary added that his Department was trying hard to do what the boy had asked—to set aside land on which to play and roam—and to conserve the human spirit.

The famous author and philosopher, Freeman Tilden, once said that "what the average man and woman love about the primeval parks is the feeling of elbow-room, bigness, far horizon, freedom. You can get these sensations in the highest degree only when the areas are large enough; and this condition is the very one that makes them of value from the scientific point of view. For the historian of the future, they must not be flooded out by river dams and 'improvements' or by other encroachments that seem at the moment of vital importance, but that later may be recognized as wasted effort and money, even commercially. For the student of plant and animal life, their value depends upon their being large enough to constitute a home. Half a home may still be a home for human beings; in the economy of the wilderness it is just about no home at all.

"Human beings are able to juggle with their environment or quit it at will for another. Only to the faintest degree is this true of the animals and plants that, with the spectacular features, constitute the attraction of the national parks."

This idea of the parks becoming a haven of refuge for citizens harried by the pace of a modern world is what John Muir envisioned so well half a century ago. He said:

"Thousands of nerve-shaken, over-civilized people are beginning to find out that going to the mountains is going home; that wilderness is a necessity; and that mountain parks and reservations are useful not only as fountains of timber and irrigating rivers, but as fountains of life."

Conservation inevitably has to include such things as scenery, recreation, and human resources, because these have to do with the well-being and happiness of people. After all, without people there is no one to understand conservation, no one to practice it, and no need for it.

Every field of human endeavor—science, education, industry—in fact, human life itself, depends on conservation. There are many forms of conservation, but that which protects the parks and shrines protects the highest aspirations of man, and is therefore said to be the highest form of conservation.

The lessons lie all around. In places that are not preserved or are not well-managed, the original beauty and inspiration sinks into mediocrity and finally into despair and poverty.

Fortunately, wise heads have prevailed and the United States still possesses in its parks vignettes of what the country was. But these are the last and only treasures, the pearls in the crown—and they must not be removed, or even chipped.

The men and women of the National Park Service know the stakes in this game of human survival. In large measure, their pride, their *esprit de corps,* their spirit of public service, comes from keeping a tremendous legacy intact to hand on to the people of the future.

The National Park Service will undoubtedly keep in tune with the times and utilize modern techniques to deal with familiar problems. There will be new tools to use in managing the parks. Insect control may be derived on a large scale from inventions in atomic radiation. New chemicals may help suppress destructive forest fires. New vehicles or aircraft may help in urgent rescue operations. Psychologists may well discover ways and means of improving visitor use and understanding of the parks. And the way the park movement is spreading worldwide, there is no end to the unfading fascination of guarding or helping to guard the world's great treasures that exist in park lands of all kinds.

In short, these times are exciting ones, and the future of the National Park Service, so long as it fulfills its mandate from the people, seems to be bright indeed. The Congress has striven to equalize the pay structure of the Federal service, making the salary of employees comparable to that of persons doing similar work outside the Government. Sick leave, vacations and other benefits are liberal—freeing the ranger and his colleagues to work and think creatively and constructively.

Wherever they are and whatever they do, the pride of the rangers and their fellow workers is contagious. It engenders in visitors an understanding and appreciation of the greatness of nature and of man. As the Rocky Mountain naturalist, Enos Mills, said: "The supreme triumph of parks is humanity . . . He who feels the spell of the wild, the rhythmic melody of falling water, the echoes among the crags, the bird songs, the wind in the pines, and the endless beat of wave upon the shore, is in tune with the universe, he will know what human brotherhood means."

In that spirit, with high standards of conduct in the public interest, and with the help and guidance of the people they serve, the National Park Service may keep the parks as Nathaniel Langford and his friends envisioned around that campfire of so long ago—public pleasuring grounds for all the people.

And so long as evening campfires burn throughout the land, so long as the park ranger stands beside these wonders of nature and of man, then will the spirit of Steve Mather be pleased. For he will know that the National Park Service is keeping the nation's heritage the way he wanted . . . safe and sound for the benefit and enjoyment of future generations.

For Further Reading

Albright, Horace, and Taylor, Frank, *Oh, Ranger!*, 1934, Dodd, Mead & Company, New York, N.Y.

Chittenden, Hiram, *Yellowstone National Park*, 1933, Stanford University Press, Stanford University, Calif., republished in 1964 by the University of Oklahoma Press, Norman, Okla.

Jensen, Paul, *National Parks*, 1964, Golden Press, New York, N.Y.

Shankland, Robert, *Steve Mather of the National Parks*, 1954, Alfred A. Knopf, New York, N.Y.

Tilden, Freeman, *The National Parks, What They Mean to You and Me*, 1951, Alfred A. Knopf, New York, N.Y.

Udall, Stewart L. *The Quiet Crisis*, 1963, Holt, Rinehart, and Winston, New York, N.Y.

Areas Administered by the National Park Service

(Cities listed are those to which mail is addressed. If no
city is shown, the park itself has a Post Office.)

Abraham Lincoln Birthplace National Historic Site, Hodgenville,
Kentucky. Traditional birthplace cabin of Abraham Lincoln.

Acadia National Park, Bar Harbor, Maine. Rugged coastal scenery.

Adams National Historic Site, Quincy, Massachusetts. Home of
Presidents John Adams and John Quincy Adams.

Allegheny Portage Railroad National Historic Site, Pennsylvania.
Where canal barge traffic was raised and lowered between 1834 and
1858.

Andrew Johnson National Historic Site, Greenville, Tennessee.
Home and grave of President Andrew Johnson.

Antietam National Battlefield Site, Sharpsburg, Maryland. Scene of
battle that ended Lee's first invarsion of the North, 1862.

Appomattox Court House National Historical Park, Appomattox,
Virginia. Site of Lee's surrender to Grant, ending Civil War, 1865.

Arches National Monument, Moab, Utah. Giant arches, windows
and pinnacles eroded from red and brown sandstones.

Aztec Ruins National Monument, Aztec, New Mexico. Excavated
and partly restored ruins of 12th-century American Indian village.

Badlands National Monument, Interior, South Dakota. Eroded
sedimentary deposits rich with prehistoric animal fossils.

Bandelier National Monument, Santa Fe, New Mexico. Ruins of
prehistoric Indian dwellings in a scenic canyon.

Bent's Old Fort National Historic Site, La Junta, Colorado. Famous
fur-trading post on the Santa Fe Trail.

Big Bend National Park, Texas. Spectacular mountain and desert
scenery along a great bend of the Rio Grande.

Big Hole National Battlefield, Montana c/o Yellowstone Park,
Wyoming. Site of 1877 battle during retreat of Chief Joseph and
Nez Perce Indians.

Black Canyon of the Gunnison National Monument, Fruita, Colorado. Awesome, sheer-walled canyon in ancient black rocks.

Blue Ridge Parkway, Virginia-North Carolina, c/o Roanoke, Virginia. Scenic parkway along 469 miles of the Blue Ridge Mountains.

Booker T. Washington National Monument, Roanoke, Virginia. Birthplace and childhood homesite of famous Negro educator.

Brices Cross Roads National Battlefield Site, Tupelo, Mississippi. Scene of 1864 battle involving General Nathan B. Forrest.

Bryce Canyon National Park, Utah. Brilliantly colored rock pinnacles, spires and walls in a giant amphitheater.

Buck Island Reef National Monument, Christiansted, Virgin Islands. Bird rookeries, tropical fishes, and magnificent coral reefs.

Cabrillo National Monument, San Diego, California. Memorial to Juan Rodriguez Cabrillo, who discovered San Diego Bay in 1542.

Canyon de Chelly National Monument, Chinle, Arizona. Prehistoric Indian ruins in a canyon on the Navajo Reservation.

Canyonlands National Park, Utah. A rugged landscape of red rock canyons, sandstone spires, arches, and other erosion features.

Cape Cod National Seashore, Eastham, Massachusetts. Open, curving beach adjacent to site of Pilgrim landing and other historic events.

Cape Hatteras National Seashore, Manteo, North Carolina. Wild beaches, waterfowl refuges and historic villages on "Outer Banks."

Capitol Reef National Monument, Torrey, Utah. Twenty-mile-long uplift of highly colored sandstone.

Capulin Mountain National Monument, Capulin, New Mexico. The symmetrical cinder cone of an extinct volcano.

Carlsbad Caverns National Park, Carlsbad, New Mexico. Giant underground chambers with countless magnificent limestone formations.

Casa Grande Ruins National Monument, Coolidge Arizona. Ruined mud or adobe tower built by Indian farmers six hundred years ago.

Castillo de San Marcos National Monument, St. Augustine, Florida. Oldest Spanish masonry fort in continental United States.

Castle Clinton National Monument, New York 4, New York. Historic immigration depot where 7½ million people entered America, 1855–90.

Cedar Breaks National Monument, Springdale, Utah. Huge natural amphitheater eroded into brightly colored sedimentary rock layers.

Chaco Canyon National Monument, Bloomfield, New Mexico. Hundreds of Indian ruins, some representing highest point of Pueblo civilization.

Chalmette National Historical Park, Arabi, Louisiana. Scene of part of the Battle of New Orleans in 1815.

Channel Islands National Monument, San Diego, California. Sea lion rookery, nesting birds, and scenic islands off Pacific coast.

Chesapeake and Ohio Canal National Monument, Maryland-West Virginia, c/o Hagerstown, Maryland. Well preserved early American canal.

Chickamauga and Chattanooga National Military Park, Georgia-Tennessee, c/o Ft. Oglethorpe, Georgia. 1863 Civil War battlefields.

Chiricahua National Monument, Dos Cabezas, Arizona. A wilderness of bizarre eroded rock shapes in Apache Indian country.

Christiansted National Historic Site, Christiansted, Virgin Islands. Waterfront buildings commemorating colonial development of islands.

City of Refuge National Historical Park, Kona, Hawaii. Sacred coastal site that protected vanquished warriors until 1819.

Colonial National Historical Park, Yorktown, Virginia. Contains Jamestown, first permanent English settlement in America, and Yorktown, scene of culminating battle of American Revolution.

Colorado National Monument, Fruita, Colorado. Sheer-walled canyons, spires, and weird formations in colorful red sandstone.

Coronado National Memorial, Hereford, Arizona. Commemorates southwestern explorations by Coronado between 1540 and 1542.

Coulee Dam National Recreation Area, Washington. Varied sports facilities on scenic Franklin D. Roosevelt Lake.

Cowpens National Battlefield Site, South Carolina, c/o Kings Mountain, North Carolina. Site of Daniel Morgan's victory over the British, 1781.

Crater Lake National Park, Medford, Oregon. Deep blue lake in extinct volcano, encircled by lava walls up to two thousand feet high.

Craters of the Moon National Monument, Arco, Idaho. Cones, caves, craters, and lava flows in a strange volcanic landscape.

Cumberland Gap National Historical Park, Kentucky-Virginia-Tennessee, c/o Middlesboro, Kentucky. Mountain pass on the Wilderness Road, explored by Daniel Boone.

Custer Battlefield National Monument, Crow Agency, Montana. Where Lt. Col. George Custer and his men were killed in 1876.

Death Valley National Monument, California. Scenic and historic desert wilderness, including lowest point in Western Hemisphere.

De Soto National Memorial, Bradenton, Florida. Commemorates the landing of De Soto in 1539 and exploration of the Southeast.

Devils Postpile National Monument, c/o Yosemite National Park, California. Close-fitting gray columns of a lava flow.

Devils Tower National Monument, Wyoming. An 865-foot-high remnant of an ancient volcanic intrusion.

Dinosaur National Monument, Utah-Colorado, c/o Vernal, Utah. Spectacular canyons and fossil deposits.

Edison National Historic Site, Orange, New Jersey. Thomas Edison's home, and the buildings and equipment he used.

Effigy Mounds National Monument, McGregor, Iowa. Outstanding Indian mounds in shapes of birds and mammals.

El Morro National Monument, Ramah, New Mexico. Inscription rock with historic carvings, including those of Spanish explorers.

Everglades National Park, Homestead, Florida. Largest remaining subtropical wilderness in the United States.

Federal Hall National Memorial, New York 4, New York. Seat of Federal Government in the early days of the Republic.

Fire Island National Seashore, New York. Stretch of relatively undeveloped shoreline off the southern coast of Long Island.

Fort Bowie National Historic Site, Arizona. Famed military post used in campaigns against the Apache Indians.

Fort Caroline National Memorial, Jacksonville, Florida. Site of 1564 French attempt to settle in the New World.

Fort Clatsop National Memorial, Astoria, Oregon. One time winter encampment of Lewis and Clark expedition.

Fort Davis National Historic Site, Fort Davis, Texas. Important fort in the struggle between Apache Indians and white settlers.

Fort Donelson National Military Park, Dover, Tennessee. Civil War fortification on the Cumberland River.

Fort Frederica National Monument, St. Simons Island, Georgia. Bastion built 1736–48 by General James Oglethorpe.

Fort Jefferson National Monument, Homestead, Florida. Wildlife sanctuary and historic fort on Dry Tortugas, Gulf of Mexico.

Fort Laramie National Historic Site, Fort Laramie, Wyoming. Fur trade post on the Oregon Trail.

Fort Larned National Historic Site, Kansas. A military post that played an important part in protecting the Santa Fe Trail.

Fort Matanzas National Monument, St. Augustine, Florida. Spanish fort built in 1737.

Fort McHenry National Monument, Baltimore, Maryland. Defense of this fort in 1814 inspired the writing of *The Star-Spangled Banner.*

Fort Necessity National Battlefield, Farmington, Pennsylvania. Site of opening battle of French and Indian War, 1754.

Fort Pulaski National Monument, Savannah Beach, Georgia. Early 19th-century fort with moat and drawbridge.

Fort Raleigh National Historic Site, Manteo, North Carolina. First English settlement, 1585, and birthplace of Virginia Dare.

Fort Smith National Historic Site, Fort Smith, Arkansas. A fort important in the protection of Indian territory.

Fort Sumter National Monument, Charleston, South Carolina. Scene of engagement beginning the Civil War.

Fort Union National Monument, Watrous, New Mexico. Ruins of early fort on the Santa Fe Trail.

Fort Vancouver National Historic Site, Vancouver, Washington. Western headquarters of Hudson's Bay Company, 1825–49.

Fredericksburg and Spotsylvania County Battlefields Memorial National Military Park, Fredericksburg, Virginia. Major Civil War battle sites.

General Grant National Memorial, New York 4, New York. Tomb of General and Mrs. Ulysses S. Grant.

George Washington Birthplace National Monument, Washington's Birthplace, Virginia. Memorial mansion and gardens.

George Washington Carver National Monument, Diamond, Missouri. Birthplace and boyhood home of famous Negro scientist.

Gettysburg National Military Park, Gettysburg, Pennsylvania. Battlefield marking the turning point of the Confederacy, and site of Lincoln's Gettysburg Address.

Gila Cliff Dwellings National Monument, Silver City, New Mexico. Ancient Indian cliff dwellings in natural caves.

Glacier National Park, West Glacier, Montana. Spectacular Rocky Mountain scenery, with numerous glaciers and lakes.

Glacier Bay National Monument, Juneau, Alaska. Majestic scenery and tidewater glaciers.

Glen Canyon National Recreation Area, Arizona-Utah, c/o Page, Arizona. Artificial lake in scenic plateau country.

Gran Quivira National Monument, Gran Quivira, New Mexico. Site of 17th-century Spanish mission.

Grand Canyon National Monument, Arizona. Contains lava dam and excellent views of the inner gorge and Colorado River.

Grand Canyon National Park, Arizona. Gigantic, colorful, mile-deep gorge of the Colorado River.

Grand Portage National Monument, Grand Marais, Minnesota. Trading post and portage route of early Indians and explorers.

Grand Teton National Park, Moose, Wyoming. Grand Teton mountain range, prairies, animal feeding grounds, "Jackson Hole" country.

Great Sand Dunes National Monument, Alamosa, Colorado. Some of the largest and highest dunes in the United States.

Great Smoky Mountains National Park, North Carolina-Tennessee, c/o Gatlinburg, Tennessee. Magnificent wilderness in southern highlands.

Guilford Courthouse National Military Park, Greensboro, North Carolina. Commemorates 1781 battle between British and Americans.

Haleakala National Park, Kahului, Hawaii. Famous volcano and colorful crater, home of rare silversword plant.

Hampton National Historic Site, Baltimore, Maryland. Georgian mansion built in late 18th century.

Harpers Ferry National Historical Park, Harpers Ferry, West Virginia. Site of famous John Brown raid and other historic events.

Hawaii Volcanoes National Park, Hawaii. Active volcanic craters of Mauna Loa and Kilauea.

Home of Franklin D. Roosevelt National Historic Site, Hyde Park, New York. Birthplace, home, and tomb of the President.

Homestead National Monument of America, Beatrice, Nebraska. Site of one of the first claims under 1862 Homestead Act.

Hopewell Village National Historic Site, Elverson, Pennsylvania. Pioneer village once devoted to iron-making.

Horseshoe Bend National Military Park, Dadeville, Alabama. Site of 1814 battle between General Jackson and Creek Indians.

Hot Springs National Park, Arkansas. Mineral hot springs used for curative purposes.

Hovenweep National Monument, Utah-Colorado, c/o Mesa Verde National Park, Colorado. Prehistoric pueblos and cliff dwellings.

Independence National Historical Park, Philadelphia, Pennsylvania. Home of the Liberty Bell, and chamber where Declaration of Independence was signed.

Isle Royale National Park, Houghton, Michigan. Large wilderness island in Lake Superior.

Jefferson National Expansion Memorial National Historic Site, St. Louis, Missouri. Commemorates territorial expansion.

Jewel Cave National Monument, Hot Springs, South Dakota. Limestone caverns with fine calcite encrustations.

John Muir National Historic Site, California. Honors the famous pioneer and literary figure who waged nationwide conservation campaigns.

Johnstown Flood National Memorial, Pennsylvania. Site of the 1889 disaster where impounded waters burst forth to destroy 2,000–3,000 lives.

Joshua Tree National Monument, Twentynine Palms, California. Wild desert land with stands of Joshua-trees.

Katmai National Monument, c/o McKinley Park, Alaska. Volcanic region, Valley of Ten Thousand Smokes, home of big brown bear.

Kennesaw Mountain National Battlefield Park, Marietta, Georgia. Where Sherman assaulted Confederate positions in 1864.

Kings Canyon National Park, Three Rivers, California. Scenic mountain wilderness in the Sierra Nevada.

Kings Mountain National Military Park, South Carolina, c/o Kings Mountain, North Carolina. Site of Revolutionary War victory, 1780.

Lake Mead National Recreation Area, Arizona-Nevada, c/o Boulder City, Nevada. Large artificial lake behind Hoover Dam.

Lassen Volcanic National Park, Mineral, California. A volcano that last erupted between 1914 and 1917.

Lava Beds National Monument, Tulelake, California. Magnificent volcanic landscape and principal site of 1873 Modoc Indian War.

Lehman Caves National Monument, Baker, Nevada. Limestone caverns richly decorated with stalactites and stalagmites.

Lincoln Boyhood National Memorial, Lincoln City, Indiana. Commemorates the younger days of the famous President.

Mammoth Cave National Park, Kentucky. 150 miles of explored passageways with pits, domes, onyx formations and underground rivers.

Manassas National Battlefield Park, Manassas, Virginia. Scene of Battles of "Bull Run," 1861 and 1862.

Mesa Verde National Park, Colorado. Most notable and best preserved prehistoric cliff dwellings in the United States.

Minute Man National Historical Park, Boston, Massachusetts. Where battles occurred on the opening day of the American Revolution.

Montezuma Castle National Monument, Camp Verde, Arizona. Five-story, 20-room cliff dwelling high in a limestone cliff.

Moores Creek National Military Park, Currie, North Carolina. Scene of Revolutionary War battle in 1776.

Morristown National Historical Park, Morristown, New Jersey. Washington's headquarters during the Revolution, 1779–80.

Mound City Group National Monument, Chillicothe, Ohio. Famous group of prehistoric Indian mounds on the Scioto River.

Mount McKinley National Park, Alaska. Highest mountain in North America, many glaciers and abundant wildlife.

Mount Rainier National Park, Longmire, Washington. Greatest single-peak glacial system in the United States.

Mount Rushmore National Memorial, Keystone, South Dakota. Colossal figures of four Presidents carved in stone.

Muir Woods National Monument, Mill Valley, California. Cathedral-like grove of giant coast redwoods.

Natchez Trace Parkway, Tupelo, Mississippi. Scenic roadway following the route of an old Indian trail.

National Capital Parks, Washington, D.C. Nearly eight hundred separate parks, large and small, in and around the nation's capital. Includes the White House, Washington Monument, Lincoln and Jefferson Memorials, Custis-Lee Mansion, and the House Where Lincoln Died.

Natural Bridges National Monument, Moab, Utah. Three sandstone bridges in wild canyon settings.

Navajo National Monument, Tonalea, Arizona. Three of the largest and most elaborate known cliff dwellings in the United States.

Ocmulgee National Monument, Macon, Georgia. Remains of prehistoric mound-builder civilization.

Olympic National Park, Port Angeles, Washington. Mountain wilderness of glaciers, rain forests, and wild animals.

Oregon Caves National Monument, Medford, Oregon. Limestone cavern high in the side of a mountain.

Organ Pipe Cactus National Monument, Ajo, Arizona. Species of cactus and other desert plants found nowhere else in the United States.

Ozark National Riverways, Missouri. Magnificent forested scenery with wild rivers, springs, caves, and sinks.

Padre Island National Seashore, Corpus Christi, Texas. Tropical beach along the edge of the Gulf of Mexico.

Pea Ridge National Military Park, Pea Ridge, Arkansas. Scene of 1862 Civil War battle.

Perry's Victory and International Peace Memorial National Monument, Put-in-Bay, Ohio. Commemorates an important 1812 naval victory.

Petersburg National Battlefield, Petersburg, Virginia. Scene of "Battle of the Crater" and longest siege in American history.

Petrified Forest National Park, Holbrook, Arizona. Natural deposit of petrified wood; portion of colorful Painted Desert.

Pinnacles National Monument, Paicines, California. Spikelike rock formations and variety of volcanic features.

Pipe Spring National Monument, Moccasin, Arizona. Historic fort and other structures built by Mormon pioneers.

Pipestone National Monument, Pipestone, Minnesota. Quarry from which Indians gathered stone for making pipes.

Platt National Park, Sulphur, Oklahoma. Numerous cold springs with distinctive mineral properties.

Point Reyes National Seashore, Point Reyes, California. Scenic geologic and historic peninsula on the Pacific coast.

Rainbow Bridge National Monument, Utah, c/o Tonalea, Arizona. Greatest known natural bridge, 309 feet high.

Richmond National Battlefield Park, Richmond, Virginia. Scene of several Civil War battles in defense of Richmond.

Rocky Mountain National Park, Estes Park, Colorado. Contains 65 peaks above 10,000 feet altitude.

Russell Cave National Monument, Bridgeport, Alabama. Cave containing almost continuous human habitation since 6,000 B.C.

Sagamore Hill National Historic Site, Oyster Bay, New York. Home of President Theodore Roosevelt.

Saguaro National Monument, Tucson, Arizona. A forest of giant saguaro cactus, unique to Arizona and Mexico.

Saint-Gaudens National Historic Site, Cornish, New Hampshire. Commemorates Augustus Saint-Gaudens, famous American sculptor (1848–1907).

St. Thomas National Historic Site, St. Thomas, Virgin Islands. Contains Fort Christian, oldest standing structure in the islands.

Salem Maritime National Historic Site, Salem, Massachusetts. Buildings associated with New England history.

San Juan National Historic Site, San Juan, Puerto Rico. Massive masonry fortification begun by the Spanish in the 16th century.

Saratoga National Historical Park, Stillwater, New York. Scene of American victory over the British in 1777.

Scotts Bluff National Monument, Gering, Nebraska. Noted landmark on the Oregon Trail.

Sequoia National Park, Three Rivers, California. Giant sequoia groves and magnificent wilderness, including Mount Whitney.

Shadow Mountain National Recreation Area, Estes Park, Colorado. Scenic lakes at the west entrance of Rocky Mountain National Park.

Shenandoah National Park, Luray, Virginia. Scenic portion of the Blue Ridge, traversed by the "Skyline Drive."

Shiloh National Military Park, Shiloh, Tennessee. Scene of Civil War battle in 1862.

Sitka National Monument, Juneau, Alaska. Stockade where Kik-siti Indians made a last stand against the Russians.

Statue of Liberty National Monument, New York 4, New York. Colossal copper statue symbolizing freedom and democracy.

Stones River National Battlefield, Murfreesboro, Tennessee. Site of a stubbornly fought Civil War battle, 1862.

Sunset Crater National Monument, Flagstaff, Arizona. Colorful volcanic cinder cone which erupted about 1066 A.D.

Theodore Roosevelt Birthplace National Historic Site, New York 4, New York. Place of the President's birth and boyhood home.

Theodore Roosevelt National Memorial Park, Medora, North Dakota. Elkhorn Ranch and scenic badlands that inspired the President.

Timpanogos Cave National Monument, American Fork, Utah. Limestone cavern in Mount Timpanogos.

Tonto National Monument, Roosevelt, Arizona. Well-preserved cliff dwellings occupied during the early part of the 14th century.

Tumacacori National Monument, Tumacacori, Arizona. Historic Spanish Catholic mission.

Tupelo National Battlefield, Tupelo, Mississippi. Commemorates a Civil War battle, July 13–14, 1864.

Tuzigoot National Monument, Clarkdale, Arizona. Prehistoric pueblo which flourished between 1000 and 1400 A.D.

Vanderbilt Mansion National Historic Site, Hyde Park, New York. Fine example of palatial American residence, 1880–1900.

Vicksburg National Military Park, Vicksburg, Mississippi. Well-preserved fortifications of 47-day siege in 1863.

Virgin Islands National Park, Charlotte Amalie, Virgin Islands. Tropical beaches, plant and animal life, and remains of colonial sugar plantations on St. John Island.

Walnut Canyon National Monument, Flagstaff, Arizona. 800-year-old cliff dwellings in a steep-walled canyon.

White Sands National Monument, Alamogordo, New Mexico. White gypsum sand dunes up to 45 feet high.

Whitman Mission National Historic Site, Walla Walla, Washington. Where Dr. Marcus Whitman ministered to the Indians.

Wind Cave National Park, Hot Springs, South Dakota. Limestone caverns famous for their boxwork formations.

Wright Brothers National Memorial, Kill Devil Hills, North Carolina. Site of first sustained flight by heavier-than-air machine.

Wupatki National Monument, Flagstaff, Arizona. Red sandstone prehistoric pueblos built by farming Indians.

Yellowstone National Park, Yellowstone Park, Wyoming. World's greatest geyser area, waterfalls, wildlife sanctuary.

Yosemite National Park, California. Spectacular mountain region of canyons, waterfalls, and giant sequoia groves.

Yucca House National Monument, c/o Mesa Verde National Park, Colorado. Unexcavated Indian ruins not open to the public.

Zion National Park, Springdale, Utah. Outstanding erosion and colorful canyon in scenic plateau.

Index